CAMPAIGN 437

CARENTAN 1944

Connecting the D-Day Beachheads

STEVEN J. ZALOGA ILLUSTRATED BY GRAHAM TURNER

OSPREY PUBLISHING
Bloomsbury Publishing Plc
Kemp House, Chawley Park, Cumnor Hill, Oxford OX2 9PH, UK
Bloomsbury Publishing Ireland Limited,
29 Earlsfort Terrace, Dublin 2, D02 AY28, Ireland
Bloomsbury Publishing Inc.
1359 Broadway, 12th Floor, New York, NY 10018, USA
E-mail: info@ospreypublishing.com
www.ospreypublishing.com

OSPREY is a trademark of Osprey Publishing Ltd

First published in Great Britain in 2026

A catalog record for this book is available from the British Library.

ISBN: PB 9781472871657; eBook 9781472871640; ePDF 9781472871671; XML 9781472871664

26 27 28 29 30 10 9 8 7 6 5 4 3 2 1

Maps by Bounford.com
3D BEVs by Paul Kime
Index by Sharon Redmayne
Typeset by Lumina Datamatics Ltd
Printed by Repro India Ltd

MIX
Paper
FSC FSC® C047271

Osprey Publishing supports the Woodland Trust, the UK's leading woodland conservation charity.

To find out more about our authors and books visit **www.ospreypublishing.com**. Here you will find extracts, author interviews, details of forthcoming events and the option to sign up for our newsletter.

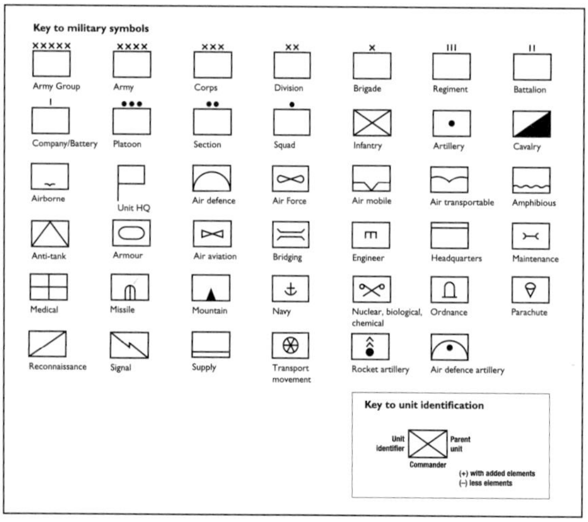

For product safety related questions contact productsafety@bloomsbury.com

Artist's note

Readers may care to note that the original paintings from which the color plates in this book were prepared are available for private sale. All reproduction copyright whatsoever is retained by the publishers. All enquiries should be addressed to: Graham Turner, PO Box 568, Aylesbury, Bucks, HP17 8EX, UK www.studio88.co.uk

The publishers regret that they can enter into no correspondence upon this matter.

Author's note

The author would like to thank Niels Henkemans, Mark Reardon, Simon Trew, Paul Woodadge, and Steven McCloud for their help in providing photos, documents and other assistance on this project. Special thanks go to Thomas Buffenbarger at the US Army Heritage and Education Center in Carlisle, PA, for his assistance while conducting research there.

The photographs in this book, unless otherwise noted, are from official US sources, including the US National Archives in College Park, MD, the US Army Heritage and Education Center (AHEC), the Special Collections at the US Military Academy at West Point, NY, and the Patton Museum at Ft. Knox, KY.

Regarding the times presented in this account, on D-Day, the Allies were on British Double Summer Time (B Time). This was Greenwich Mean Time (GMT) plus two hours. The Wehrmacht operated on the equivalent of GMT plus three or local time. For clarity, the times in this book are those used by the Allies.

For brevity, the traditional conventions have been used when referring to military units. Battalions in a regiment were identified in the fashion of 2/501st PIR (2nd Battalion, 501st Parachute Infantry Regiment). The US Army traditionally uses Arabic numerals for divisions and smaller independent formations (101st Airborne Division, 746th Tank Battalion), Roman numerals for corps (VII Corps), and spelled numbers for field armies (First US Army). For example, the 2/A/746th Tank Battalion would refer to 2nd Platoon, Company A, 746th Tank Battalion. In the case of German units, 2./GR.919 refers to the 2nd Company, Grenadier-Regiment.919; II./GR.919 indicates the 2nd Battalion of Grenadier-Regiment.919. German corps often were designated with Roman numerals, such as LXXXIV Armee Korps, but the alternate version 84.Armee Korps is used here for clarity. Field armies were designated in the fashion 7.Armee, but sometimes abbreviated in the fashion AOK.7; the former style is more commonly used here.

Glossary

AOK	Armeeoberkommando: Army high command, abbreviation for a German field army
AR	Artillerie-Regiment
Co.	Company
FJR	Fallschirmjäger Regiment: Paratrooper regiment
GIR	Glider Infantry Regiment
GR	Grenadier Regiment
GrW	Granatwerfer: mortar
Heer	German Army
HKAR	Heeres-Küsten-Artillerie-Regiment: Army coastal artillery regiment
KG	Kampfgruppe: Battlegroup
leFH	leichte Feldhaubitze: light field howitzer
Pak	Panzerabwehr Kanone: antitank gun
PIR	Parachute Infantry Regiment
Pz-Ers.u.Ausb.Abt.	Panzer-Ersatz-und-Ausbildungs-Abteilung: Tank Replacement and Training Battalion
StP	Stützpunkt: strongpoint (company-sized defense position)
tonne	Metric ton (2,205lb)
WN	Widerstandnest: defense nest (platoon-sized defense position)
z.b.V.	zur besonderen Verwendung: for special deployment

Front cover main illustration: The paratrooper charge at the Carentan causeway, June 11, 1944. (Graham Turner)
Title page photograph: Paratroopers, possibly from the 506th PIR, advance towards Carentan.

CONTENTS

ORIGINS OF THE CAMPAIGN

The battle of Carentan marked the culmination of the US Army's D-Day amphibious operation in Normandy. The Operation *Neptune* plans expected that Omaha and Utah Beaches would be connected within a day or two. This did not occur and led to a series of pitched battles between the two landing beaches lasting over a week. Carentan was at the center of these battles, since it controlled the road network between the two beachheads, as well as many of the critical river crossings.

Utah and Omaha were separated by the Vire and Douve river estuaries. The ground was marshy on the western side of the estuaries near Carentan. The Germans attempted to exploit this liquid geography by obstructing the river tributaries to further flood the area. They expected that this would limit the ability of an Allied invasion force from moving out of the beachhead into

Carentan hosts numerous commemorations every June, such as this parade of 101st Airborne Division reenactors marching through the town on June 8, 2019, on the 75th anniversary of D-Day. (Cpl. Kevin Payne, US Armed Forces Network Media Center)

the flat farmland beyond. Furthermore, the flooding would complicate any attempts at airborne landing. Carentan controlled many of the bridges and locks in the area and so was vital to this scheme.

The Operation *Neptune* plans recognized the importance of this geography. The D-Day missions of the 101st Airborne Division were to secure the causeways that provided exit from Utah Beach over the flooded areas behind the landing area. The other critical missions on D-Day were to secure the bridges and locks along the Douve River that led to Carentan. The importance of Carentan led the German 7.Armee to deploy one of its few elite units in Normandy, Fallschirmjäger-Regiment.6 (FJR.6).

The 101st Airborne Division was unable to quickly capture Carentan due to severe dispersal during the parachute drops on D-Day morning. Many troops missed their intended drop zones, and the paratroop units had considerable difficulty coalescing into organized formations due to the pre-dawn darkness and terrain difficulties. The division was not ready to advance from the drop zones toward Carentan until D+1, June 7. By this time, FJR.6 had managed to establish defensive positions in and around the town of Saint-Côme-du-Mont on the main route to Carentan. It took two days of fighting for the 101st Airborne Division to overcome the German defenses in Saint-Côme-du-Mont.

The advance from Saint-Côme-du-Mont to Carentan was hampered by the flooded areas separating the two towns. The only firm footing was a causeway that was elevated above the flooded marshes. This causeway was badly exposed to German machine-gun and artillery fire. It was so narrow that only a single battalion could approach Carentan on the road. At considerable cost, a parachute infantry battalion fought its way across the causeway on D+5, June 11. This completely undermined the German defense of Carentan and FJR.6 retreated.

Senior German commanders recognized that Carentan was essential to the defense of the Cotentin peninsula and the port of Cherbourg. As a result, the 17.SS-Panzergrenadier-Division (17.SS-Pz.Gren.Div.) was assigned to counterattack the 101st Airborne Division and regain control of Carentan. The German counterattack on D+7, June 13, was initially successful but was eventually repulsed by the intervention of the US 2nd Armored Division. By June 15, the US Army had moved the newly arrived XIX Corps into the area between Utah and Omaha Beaches, ending any further opportunities for a German operation against Carentan.

The battle for Carentan has achieved popular attention in recent years due to its depictions in two Steven Spielberg productions. It was featured in two episodes of the popular *Band of Brothers* series and also inspired the concluding scene in the film *Saving Private Ryan*, the fictional "battle of Ramelle."

CHRONOLOGY

D-Day (June 6)

0130hrs	101st Airborne Division begins parachute landings in Normandy
0600hrs	84.AK orders FJR.6 to move toward Utah Beach
0900hrs	506th PIR attacks two batteries of AR.191 at Holdy and Brécourt Manor
1900hrs	I. and II./FJR.6 deploy outside Saint-Côme-du-Mont
2100hrs	Mission *Keokuk*, a glider reinforcement consisting of 32 Horsa gliders, arrives in Landing Zone L
2200hrs	84.AK instructs FJR.6 to attack Sainte-Mère-Église the next morning
2200hrs	Gen. Taylor alerts units of 101st Airborne to attack Saint-Côme-du-Mont the following day

D+1 (June 7)

0430hrs	101st Airborne Division begins to move against Saint-Côme-du-Mont
0630hrs	Major von der Heydte changes plans and instructs FJR.6 to shift to defense of Saint-Côme-du-Mont
0900hrs	Lt. Col. Turner's 1/506th PIR leads 101st Airborne Division toward Vierville
1100hrs	Lt. Col. Strayer's 2/506th PIR reaches Angoville-au-Plain
1130hrs	Turner's 1/506th PIR reaches Beaumont
1430hrs	Squadron from 353rd Fighter Group bombs two Douve River bridges
1530hrs	Elements of Hauptmann Preikschat's I./FJR.6 clash with Capt. Shettle's 3/506th PIR detachment
1600hrs	Main body of Preikschat's I./FJR.6 ambushed by Col. Johnson's detachment near La Barquette lock

D+2 (June 8)

0445hrs	US artillery begins bombardment of Saint-Côme-du-Mont
0800hrs	Co. H, 506th PIR enters outskirts of Saint-Côme-du-Mont
1015hrs	II./FJR.6 begins retreating from Saint-Côme-du-Mont
1700hrs	FJR.6 completes retreat from Saint-Côme-du-Mont to Carentan

D+3 (June 9)

Morning	Gen. Taylor assigns 502nd PIR the mission to lead attack into Carentan via the causeway
Afternoon	Lt. Ralph Gehauf, S-2 of 3/502nd PIR, flies a reconnaissance mission over the causeway
Midnight	Lt. Col. Cole's 3/502nd PIR advanced to start of causeway at Le Pont de Douve
Midnight	101st Airborne Division artillery begins bombardment of German positions north of Carentan

D+4 (June 10)

0100hrs	1/327th GIR crosses Douve River north of Carentan
0130hrs	Lt. Gehauf leads a reconnaissance party over causeway
0700hrs	Three battalions of 327th GIR cross over Douve River and capture Brevands
Afternoon	Gehauf's patrol reaches the far side of Bridge No. 4 on the Carentan causeway

1400hrs Co. A, 1/401st GIR meet a 29th Division patrol near Auville-sur-le-Vey, the first tentative link-up of Utah and Omaha Beaches

Dusk Most of Lt. Col. Cole's 3/502nd PIR reaches Bridge No. 4

2330hrs Two Fw-190A fighter-bombers of III./Schlachtgeschwader 4 attack 3/502nd PIR on the causeway

D+5 (June 11)

0530hrs US artillery begins bombardment of German defenses near Carentan causeway

0615hrs Cole blows his whistle and starts the bayonet charge against the Ingouf farm

0900hrs 327th GIR begins to advance down the Canal de Vire et Taute toward Carentan

1000hrs Lt. Col. Cassidy begins moving the 1/502nd PIR over the causeway to reinforce Cole's 3/502nd PIR

1100hrs Two companies of II./FJR.6 counterattack paratroopers at the Ingouf farm

1600hrs Von der Heydte decides to withdraw from Carentan

Evening 506th PIR moves across the causeway through the 502nd PIR toward Hill 30

D+6 (June 12)

0500hrs 327th GIR and 501st PIR move down Canal de Vire et Taute into northern Carentan

0500hrs 506th PIR advances into Carentan from the south

0700hrs Carentan is in US hands

Afternoon 501st PIR assaults Hill 30

D+7 (June 13)

0005hrs Bradley's headquarters receive Ultra alert of German attack on Carentan

0100hrs 2nd Armored Division alerts Combat Command A (CCA) to move to Carentan

0315hrs CCA, 2nd Armored Division on the road

0530hrs 501st and 506th PIR begin to attack to the southwest

0530hrs Kampfgruppe of 17.SS-Pz.Gren.Div. begins offensive to the northeast

0600hrs 506th PIR is hit by the German attack

0630hrs 6./SS-Pz.Gren.Regt.37 attack halted by 501st PIR

0950hrs I./SS-Pz.Gren.Regt.37 reports "Attack at a standstill"

1000hrs Reinforcements from 2/502nd PIR reach 506th PIR

1030hrs CCA reaches eastern outskirts of Carentan

1415hrs CCA begins counterattack against I./SS-Pz.Gren.Regt.37

D+8 (June 14)

0600hrs CCA advances into the staging area of the German advance in an arc from Baupte to Méautis

D+9 (June 15)

Morning 30th Division of XIX Corps takes over defense of the sector between Carentan and Isigny

OPPOSING COMMANDERS

GERMAN

The supreme commander for German forces in the west (OB West, Oberbefehlshaber West) was Generalfeldmarschall Gerd von Rundstedt. His headquarters controlled three army groups in France: Heeresgruppe B on the invasion front, Heeresgruppe H in the Low Countries, and Heeresgruppe G in central and southern France. Heeresgruppe B had been commanded by Generalfeldmarschall Erwin Rommel since the autumn of 1943.

Defense of the Cotentin peninsula was assigned to the 7.Armee (AOK.7) commanded by **Generaloberst Friedrich Dollmann**. This field army controlled

On May 17, 1944, Rommel met with Generalleutnant Wilhelm Falley (left), commander of the 91.Luftlande-Division, and Major Hanns Becker (right), commander of Ost-Bataillon.439, at Château Haute in Picauville.

the French coast from the mouth of the Loire near Saint-Nazaire eastward to the Pas-de-Calais and included all German army units in Normandy and Brittany. After serving as commander of AOK.7 in the 1940 French campaign, Dollmann remained in command during the Occupation. He was in poor health and died of a heart attack on June 28, 1944, less than a month after D-Day. He was eventually replaced by General der Waffen-SS Paul Hausser.

The Basse Normandie (Lower Normandy) sector, including the Cotentin peninsula, was the responsibility of the LXXXIV.Armee Korps (84.AK) commanded by **General der Infanterie Erich Marcks**. He was assigned to the 84.AK in France on August 1, 1943 as part of the process to refresh the command structure in France with experienced Russian Front veterans. The 84.AK headquarters was located at Saint-Lô, south of Omaha Beach. Marcks was killed by an air attack on June 12, 1944; he was replaced by General Dietrich von Choltitz.

The II.Fallschirmjäger Korps under **General der Flieger Eugen Meindl** was established in Brittany in May 1944. During the course of the Carentan fighting, it was moved to the Saint-Lô area to reinforce the 84.AK. Curiously enough, for a time it was subordinate to 84.AK, an unusual situation of a corps headquarters under another corps headquarters. Meindl had been an artillery officer in World War I, serving in a mountain artillery unit at the outbreak of World War II. He switched from the Heer to the Luftwaffe paratroop force in 1940 and had his first combat jump in the 1940 landing at Narvik. His unit took part in the costly landings on Crete in 1942. He was decorated with the Knight's Cross and his skilled leadership led to his appointment as a Luftwaffe corps commander in November 1943.

The unit most closely associated with the defense of the Cotentin peninsula was the 709.Infanterie-Division (b), commanded by **Generalleutnant Karl-Wilhelm von Schlieben**. The "b" indicated *Bodenständig* (static), meaning a low mobility division intended for coastal defense. Following the D-Day landings, this division was pushed northwestward toward Cherbourg, playing little role in the Carentan fighting. In May 1944, the division was reinforced by placing the newly formed 91.Luftlande-Division behind it in the center of the Cotentin peninsula. It was commanded by Generalleutnant Wilhelm Falley, who was killed early on D-Day while returning to his headquarters from a staff exercise. He was replaced by Oberst Eugen König. An infantry battalion and two artillery batteries of this division were subordinated to Fallschirmjäger-Regiment.6 but most of the division fought north of the Carentan sector.

The unit most closely associated with the Carentan fighting was Fallschirmjäger-Regiment.6, commanded by **Major Friedrich August Freiherr von der Heydte**. He had joined

Major Friedrich August Freiherr von der Heydte, commander of Fallschirmjäger-Regiment.6.

Brigadeführer Werner Ostendorff, commander of 17.SS-Pz.Gren.Div. "Götz von Berlichingen."

the Reichswehr in 1925 and the Nazi Party in 1933, but spent most of the prewar years as a lawyer and academic. He was a cousin of Oberst Claus Graf Schenk von Stauffenberg, best known for his leadership in the assassination attempt against Hitler in July 1944. Von der Heydte served as an infantry antitank officer in the 1939 campaign in Poland, switching to the Fallschirmjäger force in 1940. An early evaluation of him described him as "a very impassioned officer characterized by flexibility, verve, and a pronounced mental attitude for operations. He relishes independent decision-making and responsibility. Open, decorous in opinions, reliable. To summarize – a personality of high warrior quality." He served as a battalion commander during the airborne landings on Crete. He commanded the Fallschirm-Lehrbataillon of the Ramcke Fallschirm-Brigade in North Africa. He was decorated with the Iron Cross in 1939 and 1940, and the Knight's Cross in 1941 for his leadership. He served on the divisional staff of the newly formed 2.Fallschirmjäger-Division but was severely injured in an aircraft accident in 1943, which required four months of hospitalization. The head of the Fallschirmjäger force, Generaloberst Kurt Student, personally recommended him for accelerated promotion and he was appointed to lead the FJR.6 in January 1944. Following the war, von der Heydte continued his legal career and served for a time in the resurrected Bundeswehr.

Arriving later in the Carentan battlefield was the 17.SS-Panzergrenadier-Division, commanded by **Brigadeführer Werner Ostendorff**. He joined the Reichswehr in 1925 and transferred to the SS in 1935. He served in SS-Division "Das Reich" as the division's chief-of-staff and held the post until June 1942, when Paul Hausser selected him as his chief-of-staff for the first Waffen-SS corps, later the II.SS-Panzer-Korps. He saw extensive combat on the Russian Front and was decorated with both classes of Iron Cross, and the Knight's Cross. Ostendorff was assigned command of the new 17.SS-Panzergrenadier-Division "Götz von Berlichingen" in January 1944. He was wounded near Carentan on June 16, 1944, temporarily giving up command. He remained with the division until late 1944, eventually being transferred in 1945 to command the 2.SS-Panzer-Division "Das Reich" in Hungary, where he died from wounds incurred in March that year.

AMERICAN

Lt. Gen. Omar Bradley commanded the First US Army at the time of the D-Day landings, including the V Corps at Omaha Beach and the VII Corps at Utah Beach. He had an exceptional group of senior officers under his command who would later rise to the highest ranks of the US Army.

The Utah Beach sector was directed by the VII Corps, led by **Maj. Gen. J. Lawton Collins**. He attended the US Military Academy at West Point and graduated 35th in the class of 1917. He commanded the 25th "Tropic Lightning" Division during the Guadalcanal campaign and received his nickname "Lightning Joe" from the division's nickname. He was one of a small number of divisional commanders transferred from the Pacific to Europe in 1944 to bring combat experience to the European Theater of Operations (ETO). Collins is widely regarded as one of the most successful US Army corps commanders of the war, famous for his exceptional leadership in Operation *Cobra* in July 1944 and the Ardennes campaign in 1944–45. Collins was Army Chief-of-Staff from August 1949 to August 1953 during the Korean War.

Maj. Gen. Maxwell D. Taylor, commander of the 101st Airborne Division, in Normandy in June 1944.

Maj. Gen. Maxwell D. Taylor commanded the 101st Airborne Division. Taylor attended West Point, graduating fourth in the class of 1922. In July 1942, Taylor became chief-of-staff of the 82nd Infantry Division, then commander of its divisional artillery after the 82nd converted to an airborne division. He served in combat with the 82nd Airborne Division on Sicily and in Italy in 1943. One of his most remarkable adventures came in late 1943 when the US Army planned an airborne operation to drop the 82nd Airborne Division near Rome to capture the city should Italy switch sides. Under Eisenhower's personal direction, he secretly traveled behind the lines to Rome to meet with Italian prime minister Marshal Pietro Badoglio. Taylor advised against the planned air drop when the Italians warned him that the Wehrmacht was moving forces into the Rome area in anticipation of an Italian defection. This cloak-and-dagger adventure prevented a major military debacle. Taylor was appointed to lead the 101st Airborne Division after its first commander, Maj. Gen. William Lee, suffered a heart attack on February 5, 1944. After the war, Taylor commanded the Eighth US Army during the final combat operations of the Korean War in late 1953, and in 1955 became the Army Chief-of-Staff. Due to his opposition to President Eisenhower's "New Look" military reforms, he became associated in later years with the Democratic Party. He was a very prominent advisor in President John F. Kennedy's and Lyndon B. Johnson's administrations during the Vietnam War.

Although Taylor was a veteran of the Sicily air-drops, most of his regimental commanders were not, due to the small number of US airborne operations prior to D-Day.

Brig. Gen. Anthony C. McAuliffe, assistant divisional commander, 101st Airborne Division.

OPPOSING FORCES

GERMAN

Fallschirmjäger-Regiment.6

Fallschirmjäger-Regiment.6 (FJR.6) was originally raised in 1943 as an independent formation but later attached to the new 2.Fallschirmjäger-Division. It took part in the seizure of Rome in September 1943. Its I./FJR.6 was deployed separately to the Russian Front in late 1943, seeing bruising combat into early 1944. The regiment was reunited in January 1944 and the decimated I./FJR.6 was rebuilt. In May 1944, the regiment was transferred to the Cotentin peninsula in Normandy to serve as the reserve of the 84.AK. It was subsequently subordinated to the 91.Luftlande-Division. Its main role was to serve as a counterweight against Allied airborne landings, even though it never received any particular training or equipment for this role. In particular, it lacked trucks and so was foot-bound and slow to move once airborne landings were conducted on D-Day.

On May 19, 1944, it had 3,457 troops; by D-Day, it probably had over 4,000 men. Unlike most German units in Normandy, the FJR.6 was composed of excellent troops recruited from Germans born within the Reich, not Volksdeutsche born outside Germany. About a third of the officers and NCOs and a fifth of the troops were combat veterans of Italy and the Russian Front. The new troops were young, with an average age of 17½. They received about four months of specialized training, including parachute jumping. A typical recruit had seven jumps ranging from 100–250m in altitude, comprising six daylight and one night jump. As in the case of US paratroopers, there was an adequate supply of volunteers and about 10 percent of the trainees were washed out when unable to meet the strict training demands.

When deployed to Normandy, the regiment was initially headquartered in L'Hôtellerie, with its I./FJR.6 near Mont Castré (subsequently Raids), II./FJR.6 in Lessay, and III./FJR.6 immediately southwest of Carentan, a distance of about 35km between each regimental location.

A Fallschirmjäger of FJR.6 mans an MG42 machine gun on a Lafette 42 mount with the antiaircraft extension amid a field of Rommel's Asparagus anti-glider obstructions in Normandy shortly before the D-Day landings in June 1944.

In a postwar report, von der Heydte explained that the regiment was so widely scattered because of Rommel's policy that such dispersion would cover a wider area to better counter Allied airborne operations than a concentrated regiment. A supply of trucks would have been a more effective solution.

The regiment was organized in a standard fashion with three battalions, each with four companies. The three Jäger companies in each battalion typically had a strength of 160–180 men, consisting of three rifle sections and a heavy section with 18 MG42 machine guns and three light or medium mortars. Each battalion had a fourth heavy company comprising a section with 12 MG42 heavy machine guns, a light gun section with 75mm guns, and a mortar section with four medium or heavy mortars. The supply of mortars appears to have been irregular and included light 50mm mortars, medium 81mm mortars, and some 120mm heavy mortars. The light gun section was supposed to be equipped with special lightweight 75mm infantry guns, but some sections had two or three 75mm Leichtgeschütze recoilless guns instead. The heavy company of III./FJR.6 had three old 50mm Pak 38 antitank guns.

A Fallschirmjäger in Normandy during the June 1944 fighting. The German paratroopers used their own pattern helmet with the truncated rim, as seen here.

The Fallschirmjäger companies were better armed than regular German infantry companies, with more machine guns and mortars. Probably their most famous weapon was the Fallschirmjäger Gewehr 42 (FG42), an advanced squad automatic weapon that entered service in the autumn of 1943. Only about 2,000 such assault rifles were manufactured by the summer of 1944, a quarter of which went to the 2.Fallschirmjäger-Division. There is some dispute about how many FG42s were in use with the FJR.6 in June 1944. One prisoner of war (PoW) interrogation indicated that they were in use in some companies, but another PoW stated that they were no longer in use with FJR.6 after the Italian campaign. Photographs show them in use in Normandy and the US Army captured some, so it remains a mystery as to who received them and how many.

Besides the Jäger battalions, the regiment included three separate companies – mortar, antitank, and Pionier (engineer). The mortar company (13.Ko.) was supposed to be equipped with the 100mm Nebelwerfer heavy mortar, but these were not available and so it was equipped with a mixture of more conventional types including the 81mm GrW 34 and 120mm GrW 42, as well as an antitank section with four 88mm Puppchen rocket launchers. The antitank company (14.Ko.) had a section with four 75mm Pak 40 towed antitanks guns, and three rocket sections, each with six 88mm Panzerschreck antitank rocket launchers, nicknamed *Ofenrohr* ('stove pipe'). However, there is some confusion in German accounts ver the term *Ofenrohr*; it most commonly did refer to the crew-served Panzerschreck, but sometimes to the disposable Panzerfaust antitank rocket. It was common practice to spread out the antitank sections, one to each battalion. Individual 75mm Pak 40

The signature weapon of the Fallschirmjäger in 1944 was the FG42 assault rifle. Only about 2,000 of this initial version were manufactured, and there is some mystery as to how many were in use with FJR.6.

The new Panzerschreck and Panzerfaust antitank rocket launchers entered service in limited numbers with German units in Normandy in the early summer of 1944. Here, a Panzerschreck 88mm rocket launcher captured from FJR.6 is being examined by US troops in the courtyard of the church in Saint-Côme-du-Mont after the fighting.

antitank guns thus did pop up during the battle, but seldom more than one at a time. Likewise, the Panzerschreck showed up in small numbers in the Jäger companies.

There were plans to add a reconnaissance and Flak company, and then use the four special companies to create a IV.Bataillon. This had not occurred by the time of the Normandy invasion, though the regiment did have a Flak section under Lt. Klein with six towed 2cm antiaircraft autocannons.

The headquarters company included a Kampfzug (combat section), bicycle section, Pionier section, and a signals section. The Kampfzug was about 40 men and consisted of experienced soldiers who could be used by the regimental commander as an emergency reserve. The bicycle section, also called the Fusilier section, was used as a reconnaissance unit but could also be employed for special assignments. The Pionier section numbered 30–40 men and its equipment included three inflatable assault rafts, six to eight flamethrowers, power-saws, demolition charges, and mines. Like most German Pionier units, it was often used as a last-ditch assault team when the situation became critical.

Comparison of US and German paratrooper companies

	German*	US**
Officers	4	8
Men	162	119
Rifles	72	106
Carbines		21
Machine pistols/SMG	43	6
Pistols	55	
Light MG	20	12
Bazookas		4
Mortars	3	3

*KStN 8121 (May 1, 1944). NB: KStN = Kriegsstärkenachweisungen, or effectively, "Table of Organization and Equipment"

**TO&E 7-35 inc. Changes (February 24, 1944)

The regiment was well-suited to airborne operations, but less well-suited to protracted ground combat. In particular, it lacked transport vehicles, with only about 70 trucks. There were roughly 50 different types on hand in June 1944, including war-booty French, Italian, and British types. This gave the regiment a lift potential of about 100 tons, but each rifle company had only two trucks each. There was a scheme to requisition French trucks and horses, but this makeshift solution was impractical and not carried out systematically in June 1944. The regiment also lacked firepower beyond its mortars, though this was partly remedied by attaching artillery units from the 91.Luftlande-Division. This became a significant problem after a few days, as the 91.Luftlande-Division was pushed northward away from Carentan immediately after D-Day, taking most of its artillery with it.

91.Luftlande-Division

The FJR.6 was subordinate to the 91.Luftlande-Division that was stationed immediately to its north. The 91.Infanterie-Division was created on January 15, 1944, at the Bitche and Baumholder training grounds. On March 15, before being completely organized, it was redesignated as the 91.Luftlande-Infanterie-Division. This was an unusual Heer air-landing division, not a Luftwaffe division as might be assumed from its name. Only one other such division, the 22.Luftlande-Division, had been formed before in 1940, but never used in its intended role. These divisions were similar in organization to a Gebirgs (mountain) light infantry division.

The revival of this type of division was intended for special operations involving the rapid insertion of infantry troops using gliders or transport aircraft. A variety of scenarios were considered, such as Operation *Hanna*, to react to an Allied landing in Denmark; Operation *Forelle*, to deal with contingencies in Hungary and on the Danube plains; and Operation *Marder*, in reaction to Allied landings on the Ligurian or Adriatic coast of Italy. Its formal mission was two-fold: first, to defend the Breton ports of Lorient and Saint-Nazaire; and second, to be ready for rapid movement by air on a mission outside of 7.Armee.

The division was intended to be deployed in eastern Brittany in three major clusters in Nantes, Redon, and Rennes, about 115km apart, for the defense of the Breton ports. This abruptly changed on May 8 while the division was still on trains from its staging areas. Instead, it was directed to change course to the Cotentin peninsula in lower Normandy, centered on La Haye-du-Puits, since the 2.Fallschirmjäger-Division was not available. One of the principal strategic concerns in Normandy was the port of Cherbourg. The 91.Luftlande-Division was wedged in between the 243.Infanterie-Division on the west coast of the peninsula and the 709.Infanterie-Division on the east coast, shielding Cherbourg from an enemy advance from the landward side.

Further details of the 91.Luftlande-Division will be limited here, since the division as a whole did not take part in the Carentan battles. Attention instead will focus on the elements of the division that did fight against the 101st Airborne Division, mainly as part of Kampfgruppe von der Heydte (KG Heydte).

Probably the most famous from the perspective of the 101st Airborne Division was Abteilung Schmidt, which was deployed to replace the I./Artillerie-Regiment.243 near Sainte-Marie-du-Mont. This detachment consisted of two of its artillery batteries, 3./AR.191 and 6./AR.191, along with a platoon of infantry from Grenadier-Regiment.1058. These two batteries were selected since they were the only ones in the division with the standard 105mm leFH 18/40 field guns, while the rest of the division's field artillery used lightweight Böhler mountain guns. The 3.Batterie was deployed at the Férme Houelbec near Holdy and the 6.Batterie at Brécourt, providing additional fire support for the strongpoints at the extreme southeast end of the 709.Infanterie-Division.

Since it was an airlanding division, Artillerie-Regiment.191 received an extremely exotic selection of field guns. Aside from the two batteries

The use of the specialized Böhler 105mm Gebirgs-Haubitze 40 instead of the usual German field gun caused considerable problems for both the 91.Luftlande-Division and Fallschirmjäger-Regiment.6 because its specialized ammunition was not readily available in the German ammo depots in Normandy.

with the standard 105mm leFH 18/40, the remainder of I./ and II./AR.191 received the 105mm Gebirgs-Haubitze 40. These were excellent, lightweight mountain howitzers, but they used their own type of 105mm ammunition that they did not share in common with standard German 105mm field howitzers. This would prove to be a major problem as the division was short of ammunition, and mountain howitzer ammunition was not readily available in Normandy ammunition depots. The III./AR.191 was armed with 88mm antitank guns as improvised field artillery.

The other element of the 91.Luftlande-Division eventually assigned to von der Heydte was Major Diekhoff's III./GR.1058. This was the southern-most battalion of the division headquartered in Saint-Côme-du-Mont, immediately north of Carentan. This was not initially attached to KG Heydte but was added due to circumstances, as described later. As of May 13, 1944, III./GR.1058 had 696 officers and men, 135 horses, and 43 vehicles. By the time of D-Day, the 91.Luftlande-Division was not fully manned or equipped, though better than other units in Normandy.

On average, about half the troops in the division had some combat experience, while the rest were new recruits. By 1944, the Wehrmacht was facing a severe shortage of personnel and often had to make do with substandard recruits. The commander of 3./GR.1058 despaired over the quality of the troops in his company:

> My personnel were pitiful, including a man with a crippled hand. Two of them were short-sighted – terrible! They couldn't shoot at all. They couldn't even recognize a man 30 meters away. None of them belonged to a sports club, none of them were Party members, none of them belonged to a gymnastics club; [only] two of them had a sports badge, I think. The average age consisted, on the one hand, of quite young people, 18- and 19-year-olds, who were not fully developed and without any strength, completely weak people; and, on the other hand, of older men over 35, 38 years old, who were overworked, family men. The NCOs had been raked up from the district headquarters, railway station guards and transport commands, and the devil only knows where they all came from. The situation was this: In all sections we had MGs, grenade launchers, semi-automatic rifles and sniper rifles.

Good God! To whom shall I give these highly specialized weapons? When I give someone a semi-automatic rifle or grenade launcher, then I need someone who can think and act by himself and knows how to handle the weapon. Our training was extremely bad. I always felt more like a duty NCO, not like a company commander.

The only armored support in the area for the first week was Panzer-Ersatz-und-Ausbildungs-Abteilung.100 (Tank Replacement and Training Battalion 100), headquartered in Baupte and so adjacent to two of the FJR.6 battalions and III./GR.1058. It was assigned to the 91.Luftlande-Division and had 46 tanks, mainly war-booty French models including the obsolete R35, H39, and B1 bis along with a few PzKpfw IIIs. Of these tanks, only 17 were operational and another ten marginally functional in an emergency. The operational tanks were consolidated into the 3.Kompanie that took part in a famous attack against the 82nd Airborne Division at La Fière bridge as part of a 91.Luftlande-Division assault. However, the remaining companies provided no help to FJR.6. Von der Heydte was scathing about their timid performance at the time of the Carentan fighting, when they retreated to Baupte. The battalion commander was later arrested for dereliction of duty.

Other Heer units

There were several Ost-Bataillone in the area, of which two, Ost-Bataillon.439 and Ost-Bataillon.635, were eventually attached to FJR.6. These units were formed from Soviet PoWs, commanded by German officers. In 1943, Berlin had transferred 20 German infantry battalions from the West to the Russian Front, exchanging them for 60 of these Eastern battalions. Ost-Bataillon.439 had been formed in November 1942 and sent to France in October 1943. It was initially assigned to Grenadier-Regiment.726 of the 716.Infanterie-Division. Ost-Bataillon.635 had been formed in 1942 and sent to France in late 1943. It was originally part of the Ost-Grenadier-Regiment z.b.V.752 (z.b.V.: zur besonderen Verwendung, "for special deployment") defending the western Cotentin coast near Granville. German officers were skeptical of the loyalty of these units and avoided placing them in critical locations except in emergencies.

The 91.Luftlande-Division had 160 Kettenkrad tracked motorcycles for logistical support. The 506th PIR captured numerous examples, and this one was being used to haul water to forward positions near Carentan.

17.SS-Panzergrenadier-Division "Götz von Berlichingen"

One of the divisions arriving in the Cotentin area after the start of the invasion was the 17.SS-Panzergrenadier-Division. It was created in October 1943 near Poitiers, France. By June 1, 1944, it had 17,321 men but was short of 233 officers and 1,541 NCOs, or about 40 percent of its leadership ranks. Due to its late formation, it was forced to draw heavily on Volksdeutsche recruits – ethnic Germans from various areas, including Romania, Hungary, and Yugoslavia, as well as Germans from Alsace. Von der Heydte offered a scathing assessment of the unit:

> Although the division was well-armed and well-equipped, it was surprisingly poorly trained. The majority of the officers had neither the training nor combat experience to enable them to fill their positions adequately ... lacking the elementary knowledge of tactics required of an officer-candidate. The low standard of training of the division's artillery officers was particularly noticeable... The [division's] artillery was not able to flexibly concentrate its fire in brief bursts after observation, or to fire ahead of advancing infantry... [It] usually fought a "private war" without paying any attention to the infantry.

Like most Panzergrenadier divisions at this stage of the war, its Panzer regiment was not equipped with tanks, but with assault guns. It was issued with the lesser-known StuG IV instead of the more common StuG III, and these would play a prominent role in the Carentan fighting. As of June 1, it had 37 of its authorized 42 StuG IVs on hand. Its Panzerjäger battalion had a company of Marder tank destroyers, three of which were the old Marder III (7.62cm) and the remainder the Marder III (75mm Pak 40).

Although its "Panzergrenadier" designation might imply its use of armored half-tracks, that was not the case and all of its Panzergrenadier units nominally motorized used trucks. Its most serious equipment shortage was in trucks, having only 245 of an authorized 1,696. As a result, some of its battalions were obliged to use bicycles or expropriated French civilian trucks for movement. It was better equipped with PKW (Personenkraftwagen) passenger cars, having 763, or about three-quarters of the authorized amount. It was at or near authorized strength in most weapon categories and had a few oddball types, including 33 old 50mm Pak 38 antitank guns, 15 28mm antitank guns, and 20 war-booty Soviet 76mm infantry guns.

This Marder III on the right of SS-Panzerjäger-Abt.17 was knocked out during the fighting outside Carentan on June 13, with the left side of its armored shield smashed in. The war-booty Hotchkiss H39 was from Pz-Ers.u.Ausb. Abt.100 based near Baupte, and subordinate to the 91.Luftlande-Division.

AMERICAN

SS-Panzer-Abt.17 was equipped with the StuG IV assault gun instead of the more common StuG III. This one was knocked out during the fighting outside Carentan on June 13 and is seen here being towed by a US Army wrecker.

The principal US Army unit involved in the battle of Carentan was the 101st Airborne Division. It was raised at Camp Claiborne, Louisiana, in August 1942, based around the 327th and 401st Glider Infantry Regiments (GIR) and 502nd Parachute Infantry Regiment (PIR). As will be noticed, the initial division configuration favored glider over parachute regiments. The ideal mix of paratroop versus glider units was controversial. Initially, the Army Ground Forces headquarters favored a higher percentage of glider battalions because the glider troops did not require specialized jump training and the gliders promised to be cheap and reusable. From a tactical perspective, the early combat drops such as Sicily demonstrated the tendency of paratroop units to become badly scattered, leading to poor unit assembly and failed missions. Gliders promised to circumvent these problems because the unit arrived intact at the small unit (squad) level. Gliders promised that dispersion could be better controlled. In addition, gliders made it possible to land larger equipment such as jeeps, light artillery, and supplies in a more convenient fashion than by parachute. On the other hand, gliders took up more air time for delivery of a unit due to the spacing requirements of the gliders and the need for more relaxed formation flying to prevent midair collisions between tow planes and gliders. Time was a critical ingredient in airborne operations, as the enemy forces were alerted once the drops began and antiaircraft fire increased once surprise was lost. This factor thus favored parachute infantry.

As a result of these considerations, the division was reorganized in early 1944. It had three PIRs on D-Day, but the two glider regiments were trimmed back. Two battalions of the 327th GIR remained with the 101st Airborne Division, while the 401st GIR was split in two, with the 1/401st GIR remaining with the 101st Airborne and the 2/401st GIR transferred to the 82nd Airborne Division. Due to a shortage of gliders in England at the time, it was decided that the 327th/401st GIRs would be landed by sea on June 6–7, with the exception of some headquarters and antitank troops who would be landed by glider.

The troops of the 327th GIR were equipped much the same as normal US infantry, without the distinctive paratrooper equipment. These two glidermen are Pvt. Earl Parker and Richard Hochstetler, pictured outside Carentan following the capture of the town. On their helmet is the shamrock insignia of the 327th GIR.

The US Army recognized that paratroop units would have to be manned by elite troops. Jumping out of an aircraft at low altitude on a pitch-dark night, burdened with nearly 100lb of gear, and being ready to fight on reaching the ground were extreme demands not expected of ordinary infantry conscripts. Paratroop operations often resulted in small units being widely scattered, and the troops needed a high degree of self-motivation and initiative to carry out their

Three men of the 101st Airborne Division inspect a German MP40 machine pistol captured during the fighting near Carentan. From left to right they are Pvt. Garland More, Pvt. Edward Olstowski, and Pvt. Larry Pablett. More and Olstowski are wearing the M1942 airborne jump suit, while Pablett is not, suggesting he was not a member of one of the parachute regiments.

mission. As a result, the US Army decided that paratroopers would be volunteers. Many adventurous young soldiers were attracted by the allure of joining an elite combat force, and *esprit-de-corps* was consciously fostered by the paratroop commanders by distinguishing the paratroopers from regular infantry troops with modified battle-dress, jump boots, and distinctive insignia. Other incentives were offered, such an additional $50 per month in jump pay ($100 for officers).

In contrast to the paratroopers, little separated the glider infantry, or "glider riders," from ordinary infantry. They did not receive jump training, their equipment was essentially the same as regular infantry, and they did not receive any hazardous-duty pay. The distinct differences in treatment between the glider infantry and the paratroop infantry in the airborne divisions fostered resentment in the glider ranks. A poster appeared at one of the army bases with gruesome photos of several glider wrecks and the slogan: "Join the Glider Troops! No Flight Pay, No Jump Pay, But Never a Dull Moment." The situation became alarming enough that on July 1, 1944, after the D-Day operations, the US Army reversed its policy and awarded extra glider pay.

Although most of the troops of the 101st Airborne had not seen combat prior to Normandy, their training was exceptionally thorough. German commander von der Heydte later remarked that the marksmanship of the paratroopers was so good that it was more feared by his Fallschirmjäger troops than American artillery. This became even more evident later in the campaign when facing regular US infantry divisions that did not demonstrate such a high level of marksmanship.

Organic fire support for the airborne divisions was provided by the M1A1 75mm pack howitzer on an M8 carriage that could be broken down into multiple loads for parachute delivery or carried in a glider. This M1A1 is on exhibit at the Air Mobility Command Museum at Dover Air Force Base, Delaware. (Author)

ORDER OF BATTLE

GERMAN

Fallschirmjäger-Regiment.6	**Major Friedrich August von der Heydte**
I.Bataillon	Hauptmann Emil Preikschat
II.Bataillon	Hauptmann Rolf Mager
III.Bataillon	Hauptmann Horst Trebes
13.Granatwerfer-Kompanie	Oberleutnant Nahde
14.Panzerjäger-Kompanie	Leutnant Geck
15.Pionier-Kompanie	Hauptmann Hauch

AMERICAN

101st Airborne Division	**Maj. Gen. Maxwell D. Taylor**
101st Pathfinder Company (Provisional)	Capt. Frank L. Lillyman
327th Glider Infantry Regiment	**Col. George S. Wear (relieved June 10, 1944), Col. Joseph H. Harper**
1st Battalion	Lt. Col. Hartford T. Salee (WIA June 10, 1944)
2nd Battalion	Lt. Col. Thomas J. Rouzie
1st Battalion, 401st GIR	Lt. Col. Ray C. Allen
501st Parachute Infantry Regiment	**Col. Howard R. Johnson**
1st Battalion	Lt. Col. Robert C. Carroll (KIA June 6, 1944), Lt. Col. Harry W.O. Kinnard
2nd Battalion	Lt. Col. Robert A. Ballard
3rd Battalion	Lt. Col. Julian J. Ewell
502nd Parachute Infantry Regiment	**Col. George Van Horn Moseley, Jr. (WIA June 6, 1944), Lt. Col. John H. Michaelis**
1st Battalion	Lt. Col. Patrick F. Cassidy
2nd Battalion	Lt. Col. Steven A. Chapuis
3rd Battalion	Lt. Col. Robert G. Cole
506th Parachute Infantry Regiment	**Col. Robert Sink**
1st Battalion	Lt. Col. William L. Turner (KIA June 7, 1944), Lt. Col. James L. LaPrade
2nd Battalion	Lt. Col. Robert L. Strayer
3rd Battalion	Lt. Col. Robert Lee Wolverton (KIA June 6, 1944), Maj. Oliver M. Horton
Divisional Artillery	
321st Glider Field Artillery Battalion	Lt. Col. Edward L. Carmichael
377th Parachute Field Artillery Battalion	Lt. Col. Benjamin Weisberg
907th Glider Field Artillery Battalion	Lt. Col. Clarence F. Nelson
81st Airborne Antiaircraft Battalion	Maj. X.B. Cox, Jr.
Engineers	
326th Airborne Engineer Battalion	Lt. Col. John C. Pappas (KIA June 13, 1944), Maj. Hugh A. Mozley
Attachments	
65th Armored Field Artillery Battalion	Lt. Col. Edward A. Bailey
70th Tank Battalion	Lt. Col. John C. Welborn

OPPOSING PLANS

GERMAN

German planning for the defense of France was tortuous due to disharmony over where the Allies were expected to land. The consensus was that the Pas-de-Calais was the most likely location since it was nearest to the English ports. By the spring of 1944, there were dissenting voices, most notably the Kriegsmarine. Luftwaffe reconnaissance in early 1944 over the Portsmouth–Plymouth area led Kriegsmarine analysts to argue that Normandy was a likely site. Other prominent organizations such as the intelligence agency Fremde Heere West (Foreign Armies West) and the OKW (Oberkommando der Wehrmacht) disagreed and still felt that the Pas-de-Calais was most likely. One of the few points of consensus was that the Allies would attempt to secure a major port, with Brest, Cherbourg, Le Havre, and Boulogne considered potential objectives.

On April 26, 1944, Hitler intervened and instructed that more resources should be directed to Normandy and Brittany, probably influenced by the Kriegsmarine assessment. When OB West retorted that it lacked the resources, on May 6, Hitler ordered Generaloberst Alfred Jodl, the Chief of the Operations Staff of the OKW, to make it clear to Generalfeldmarschall Gerd von Rundstedt, the OB West, that "the Cotentin peninsula would be the enemy's first target." The Cotentin peninsula included the port of Cherbourg. Hitler did not believe that the Cotentin would be the only Allied landing point, rather that the Cotentin peninsula or Brittany would be the bridgehead and might be followed by the main landings elsewhere.

Hitler's intervention in early May led to a significant reinforcement of the Cotentin peninsula in Normandy. Until the spring of 1944, it had been defended by the 709.Infanterie-Division (b) on the eastern side and the 243. Infanterie-Division on the western side. In mid-May, the 91.Luftlande-Division was added, positioned in the center of the Cotentin, and therefore able to support operations on either side of the peninsula. Another addition was the Fallschirmjäger-Regiment.6, subordinated to the 91.Luftlande-Division, and positioned to cover the Douve and Vire estuaries at the base of the peninsula. River estuaries were considered attractive landing sites because they could be used to move troops and supplies inland via the riverways and canals.

German strategists believed that the Allies were more likely to seize the port of Cherbourg from the landward side, rather than a direct frontal landing on the coast. This was in part due to the rocky coastal terrain on either side of Cherbourg that was not suitable for amphibious operations. The Atlantikwall fortifications and gun batteries added between 1942 and 1944 further discouraged Allied landings on the Cherbourg coast. The most likely Allied tactical approach was to conduct a landing on the Cotentin coast, then quickly surge across the narrow peninsula before turning north to lay siege to Cherbourg from the landward side. This was indeed the Allied plan.

In view of past experiences in the Mediterranean theater, the German outlook about an Allied invasion of France was pessimistic. Most German commanders felt that the Allies were likely to gain a beachhead. The main contest would come afterwards, when the beachhead would be counterattacked by reserves held further inland. This tactical approach had been attempted in Sicily, at Salerno, and at Anzio, and in each case had failed. This was noted by Rommel, who argued that the Allies had to be stopped at the shoreline and thrown back into the sea immediately. He believed the Germans could not wait for a counterattack. Other German commanders were dubious of this approach, as the French coastline was too long to create formidable defenses everywhere.

The Atlantikwall on the Cotentin coast was not as intimidating as in the Pas-de-Calais, but it did have an impressive array of coastal batteries in the Azeville–Crisbecq area, near the future Utah Beach. Since this could not be quickly reinforced, Rommel pushed for further troop concentrations rather than more concrete to improve defenses. Among his requests was the deployment of the 12.SS-Panzer-Division near the Douve and Vire estuaries, a proposal that was rejected by both OKW and OB West.

German strategists expected that any Allied landings in Normandy would be accompanied by airborne landings, as had occurred on Sicily and at Salerno. This was one reason for the deployment of Fallschirmjäger-Regiment.6, as Rommel felt that the dispersion of its three battalions would cover a larger area and therefore be more suitable for the anti-airborne mission.

OB West, having been concerned about the airborne threat since 1943, had released an instruction guide on anti-airborne tactics in April that year, *Merkblatt für Abwehr von Fallschirm (FS und Luftlande) Truppen.* It suggested a variety of defense measures and tactics. Potential landing sites

In February 1944, German engineer troops from Festungs-Pionier-Stab.11 used sandbags to block the La Madeleine River in Baupte, upstream from Carentan, as part of the program to create flooded areas to discourage the Allied use of gliders.

Rommel encouraged the use of timber obstacles in fields to discourage the Allied use of gliders. Here is a field in Normandy after D-Day dotted with Rommel's Asparagus, with a crashed CG-4A glider amid the obstacles.

were to be obstructed by obstacles and minefields. Important installations had to be defended from all sides, not simply toward the coast. Observation posts such as church steeples were a key requirement to find the location of enemy airborne forces during the operation. Mobile reserves were also essential since the location of an airborne attack was unpredictable.

Rommel himself came up with the concept for *Luftlandhindernis* (airlanding obstacles) consisting of 2.5m-long wooden poles, linked with wire and occasionally festooned with mines or other explosive devices. These were dubbed *Rommelspargel* (Rommel's Asparagus). The Festungs-Pionier-Stab.11 oversaw the installation of over 375,000 of these posts in the 7.Armee sector of Normandy. This was not as impressive as it might seem, as the instructions called for a thousand poles per square kilometer. These obstacles were not especially common on the Cotentin peninsula, the Atlantikwall programs monopolizing timber.

A more consequential program was started in July 1943 to utilize water-obstacles. The Cotentin peninsula was full of marshlands and was naturally prone to seasonal flooding. Indeed, Carentan's full name is Carentan-les-Marais (Carentan of the Marshes). The French government had already created an extensive set of canals and locks to control river flow in the

The Carentan area is subject to periodic spring floods, which provide a good analog of the effects of the deliberate flooding of the area by the Wehrmacht in 1944. These farm fields near Liesville-sur-Douve in February 2025 have been completely inundated, leaving small islands of passable terrain. (Paul Woodadge)

Carentan area. Aside from taking control of these systems for military purposes, the Festungs-Pionier-Stab.11 began blocking streams in the winter of 1944 to trap spring rain. There were two principal goals of the program: to flood the area immediately behind the coastline to make exit off the beaches difficult and to flood flat farm fields that might otherwise be attractive glider landing sites. In April 1944, the program was expanded to create an almost continuously flooded zone from Sainte-Mère-Église all the way to Isigny. As will become evident in the discussion of the campaign, this program of water obstacles proved to be a double-edged sword, arguably having a more deleterious effect on Wehrmacht units than on the US Army.

AMERICAN

The principal operational role for the VII Corps after securing Utah Beach was to turn northward and capture Cherbourg. Although the Allies planned to erect artificial Mulberry harbors off the Normandy coast, a functioning port would be enormously helpful for Allied logistics. The original objective was to secure Cherbourg by D+14.

On April 26, 1944, the Allies' Ultra signals intelligence organization decrypted an order from OKW chief-of-staff Generaloberst Alfred Jodl regarding reinforcements for Normandy. It identified the 91.Luftlande-Division and Fallschirmjäger-Regiment.6 as two of the units destined for Normandy. Another series of decrypts from May 24–27 indicated that the 243.Infanterie-Division had been moved northward to protect the southwest coast of the Cotentin peninsula, the 91.Luftlande-Division was wedged between the 243.Infanterie-Division and the 709.Infanterie-Division (b), and FJR.6 had been placed in the Carentan area. This required a hasty reconfiguration of Allied plans, since the original scheme had the 82nd Airborne Division landing near La Haye-du-Puits to quickly seal off the Cotentin peninsula. However, this was no longer viable in view of the extensive German reinforcement of this area. Consequently, the new plans placed both the 82nd and 101st Airborne Divisions immediately behind the Utah Beach area. The date for capturing Cherbourg was pushed back to D+15 due to Allied intelligence having discovered the addition of new German units on the Cotentin peninsula. Nevertheless, it was expected that Carentan would be captured on D+1.

The slow progress to create a junction of the VII Corps at Utah Beach and the V Corps at Omaha Beach led Gen. Dwight Eisenhower on D+2, June 8, to instruct VII Corps to shift its short-term focus from Cherbourg to Carentan. Eisenhower was troubled that there was a significant gap between the two American beachheads, which made them a lucrative objective for the growing number of German divisions arriving in Normandy.

Further Ultra decrypts indicated that the Germans were substantially reinforcing the units defending Cherbourg by transferring units from Brittany. Rather than follow the original plan of a single-division drive toward Cherbourg, on June 9 (D+3) Collins decided it would be necessary to cut off the Cotentin peninsula to prevent further German reinforcement of the Cherbourg front prior to a multi-division assault on the port. This led to further pressure to capture Carentan as a prerequisite for the eventual effort to cut off the Cotentin peninsula.

THE CAMPAIGN

PRELUDE TO CARENTAN

Albany Mission

The 101st Airborne Division began landing around 0130hrs on D-Day, June 6, 1944. The division's initial air-landings were codenamed the Albany Mission. The primary objective was to seize control of the area behind Utah Beach to facilitate the exit of the 4th Infantry Division from the beach later by securing the causeways that crossed the flooded areas immediately behind the beach. The secondary mission was to protect the southern flank of VII Corps by destroying two bridges on the Carentan highway and a railroad bridge west of it, gaining control of La Barquette lock, and establishing a bridgehead over the Douve River northeast of Carentan. The control of the bridges was undertaken to shut out all enemy reinforcements to the battle zone from the south.

The 502nd PIR and 506th PIR were assigned to the primary objective. Most of the 2/502nd PIR was dropped compactly but inaccurately on the far edge of Drop Zone C, 3 miles south of the intended Drop Zone A. In spite of the confusion, a scouting patrol moved on the German coastal battery at Saint-Martin-de-Varreville. This was 1./HKAR.1261, with four war-booty Soviet 122mm A-19 field guns enclosed in Regelbau 669 casemates. These guns had a range of about 20km, threatening the landing ships off Utah Beach. Due to this substantial threat, the site had been bombed on the night of May 28/29 by 64 RAF Lancasters, which delivered 356 tons of bombs. This destroyed one gun and casemate and damaged two more. As a result, the battery moved its surviving guns further back 600m from the coast, but without any fortified cover. The site was struck again in the early hours of June 5/6 by another RAF raid, pulverizing the location with a further 613 tons of bombs. Shortly before dawn, the site was struck once more by 90 US 9th Tactical Air Force B-26 Marauders dropping 123 tons of bombs. By the time that a paratrooper scouting patrol reached the smoldering ruins, it had been abandoned by its crews.

This was one of the 105mm leFH 18/40M field howitzers of 3.Batterie/AR.191 near the Férme Houelbec in Holdy that was captured on D-Day by a group of paratroopers under Capt. Lloyd Patch of HQ, 1/506th PIR, and Capt. Knut Raudstein of Co. C, 506th PIR.

The bulk of the 2/502nd PIR moved on to its next objective, the western side of the Audouville-la-Hubert causeway (Exit 3), arriving there around 0730hrs and ambushing troops of GR.919, 709.Infanterie-Division retreating from the beach. The 1/502nd PIR landed near Saint-Germain-de-Varreville, with 20 of the 36 aircraft within a mile of the pathfinder beacon. The 1/502nd PIR held the northern perimeter through D-Day, fighting a number of skirmishes with German troops and sending detachments to link up with the 82nd Airborne near Sainte-Mère-Église. The 377th Parachute Field Artillery was badly dispersed during its landings, and only a single 75mm howitzer was put into action on D-Day.

Two battalions of the 506th PIR landed in Drop Zone C. The C-47 transport aircraft passed over a concentration of German flak near Étienville. In spite of the fire, some drops were concentrated, with one serial of 14 aircraft dropping almost on top of Drop Zone C, and another serial of 13 bunching their sticks 1½ miles east and southeast of the drop zone. But the other serials ended up much further from their intended targets due to confusion over the pathfinder beacons. Some 140 men of the HQ and 1/506th PIR assembled in the regimental area in the first hours of the landing. The regimental commander, Col. Robert Sink, established a command post in Culoville. The 2/506th PIR landed north of the drop zone and two disconnected groups set out to secure the Houdienville (Exit 2) and Pouppeville (Exit 1) causeways. Delayed by frequent skirmishes with German troops, the detachments did not arrive near the beach until the 4th Infantry Division was already moving inland over the causeways from the landing beaches.

Next to land was the 3/501st PIR and the divisional HQ, which was to control the planned glider landing area near Hiesville. Gen. Taylor, not in contact with the 506th PIR, sent another detachment to the Pouppeville Exit 1 causeway. This was the first of the three paratrooper columns to actually reach the causeway around 0800hrs, but it took nearly four hours

Much of the fire support for the 101st Airborne Division on D-Day and the next few days came from the cruiser USS *Quincy*.

EXPANDING THE UTAH BEACH BRIDGEHEAD, JUNE 6, 1944

101st Airborne Division and 4th Infantry Division push out of Utah Beach.

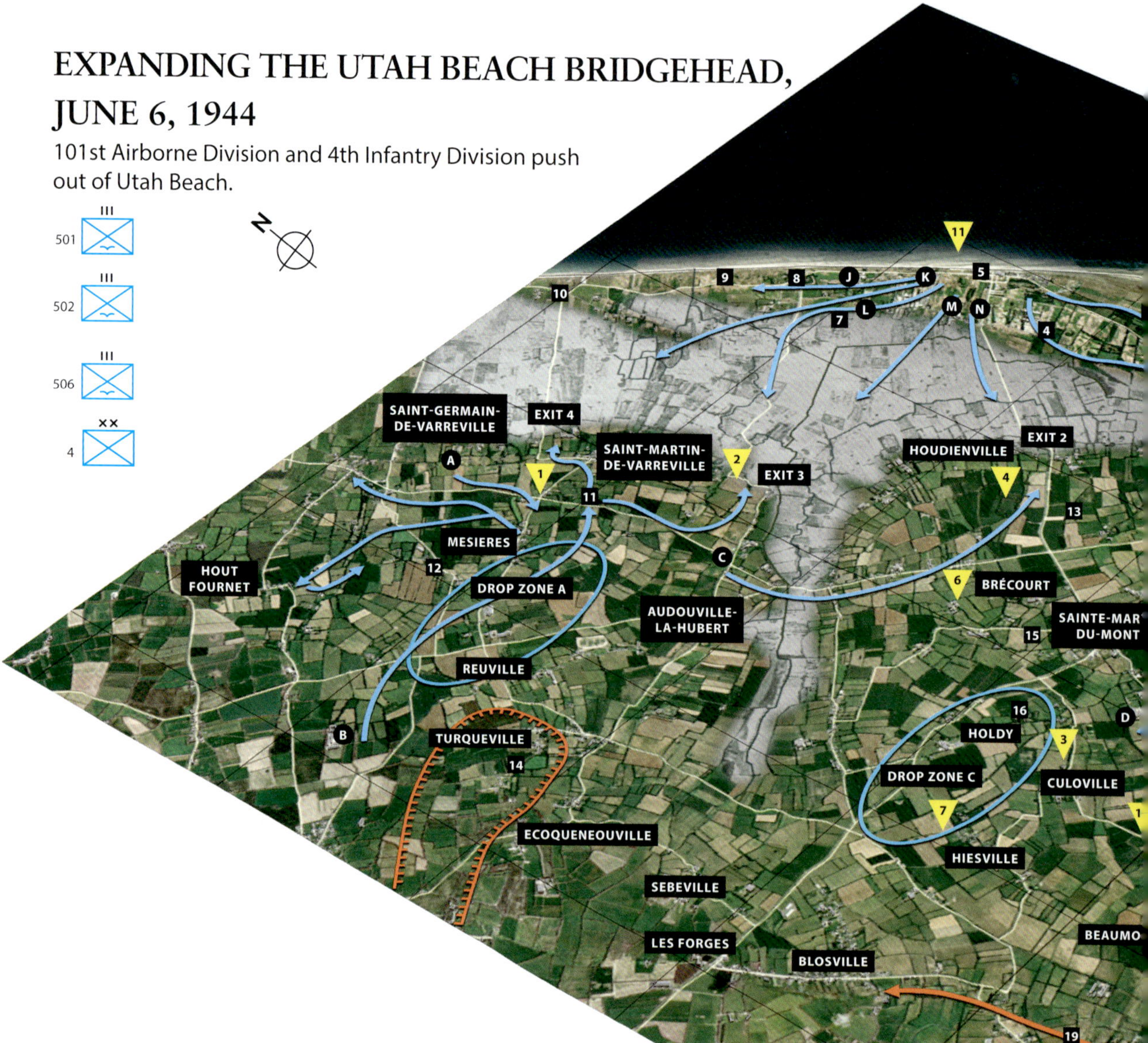

EVENTS

1. The German 122mm coastal gun battery, 1./HKAR.1261, at Saint-Martin-de-Varreville is bombed in the early hours of June 5/6 by an RAF raid as part of Operation *Flashlamp* with 613 tons of bombs. It is hit again by 90 B-26 Marauders with a further 123 tons of bombs shortly before dawn. US paratrooper scouts find it a smoldering ruin.

2. The bulk of the 2/502nd PIR reaches the Audouville-la-Hubert causeway (Exit 3) around 0730hrs, and ambush a German platoon from GR.919 retreating from the beach.

3. A company-strength detachment of 140 men of the HQ and 1/506th PIR under Col. Robert Sink establishes a command post in Culoville.

4. The 2/506th PIR secures the Houdienville (Exit 2) and Pouppeville (Exit 1) causeways from Utah Beach, meeting the 4th Infantry Division.

5. Gen. Taylor with the 3/501st PIR and the divisional HQ send another detachment to the Pouppeville (Exit 1) causeway around 0800hrs.

6. Paratroopers under Lt. Dick Winters of Co. E, 506th PIR, overwhelm the 6.Batterie/AR.191 near Brécourt Manor.

7. The 3.Batterie/AR.191 near the Férme Houelbec in Holdy is captured by a group of paratroopers under Capt. Lloyd Patch of HQ, 1/506th PIR, and Capt. Knut Raudstein of Co. C, 506th PIR.

8. Elements of 1/501st PIR under Col. Howard R. Johnson take control of La Barquette lock, which controlled the flooding of the areas along the Douve River.

9. Lt. Col. Robert Ballard's 2/501st PIR spends most of the day fighting around Les Droueries with elements of the III./GR.1058.

10. Capt. Shettle's detachment from 3/506th PIR secures the two bridges over the Douve.

11. The 4th Infantry Division lands against weak resistance and proceeds to exit the beachhead area over the causeways in regimental groups.

12. Around 1100hrs, Major von der Heydte reaches Saint-Côme-du-Mont and places Major Diekhoff's III./GR.1058 of the 91.Luftlande-Division under his command.

13. Preikschat's I./FJR.6 arrives near Saint-Côme-du-Mont in the early afternoon and von der Heydte directs them toward the northeast to block the beach exits.

14. Mager's II./FJR.6 also advances out of Saint-Côme-du-Mont around 1900hrs, oriented toward Hiesville, skirmishing with advancing US paratroopers.

Note: gridlines are shown at intervals of 2km (1.24 miles).

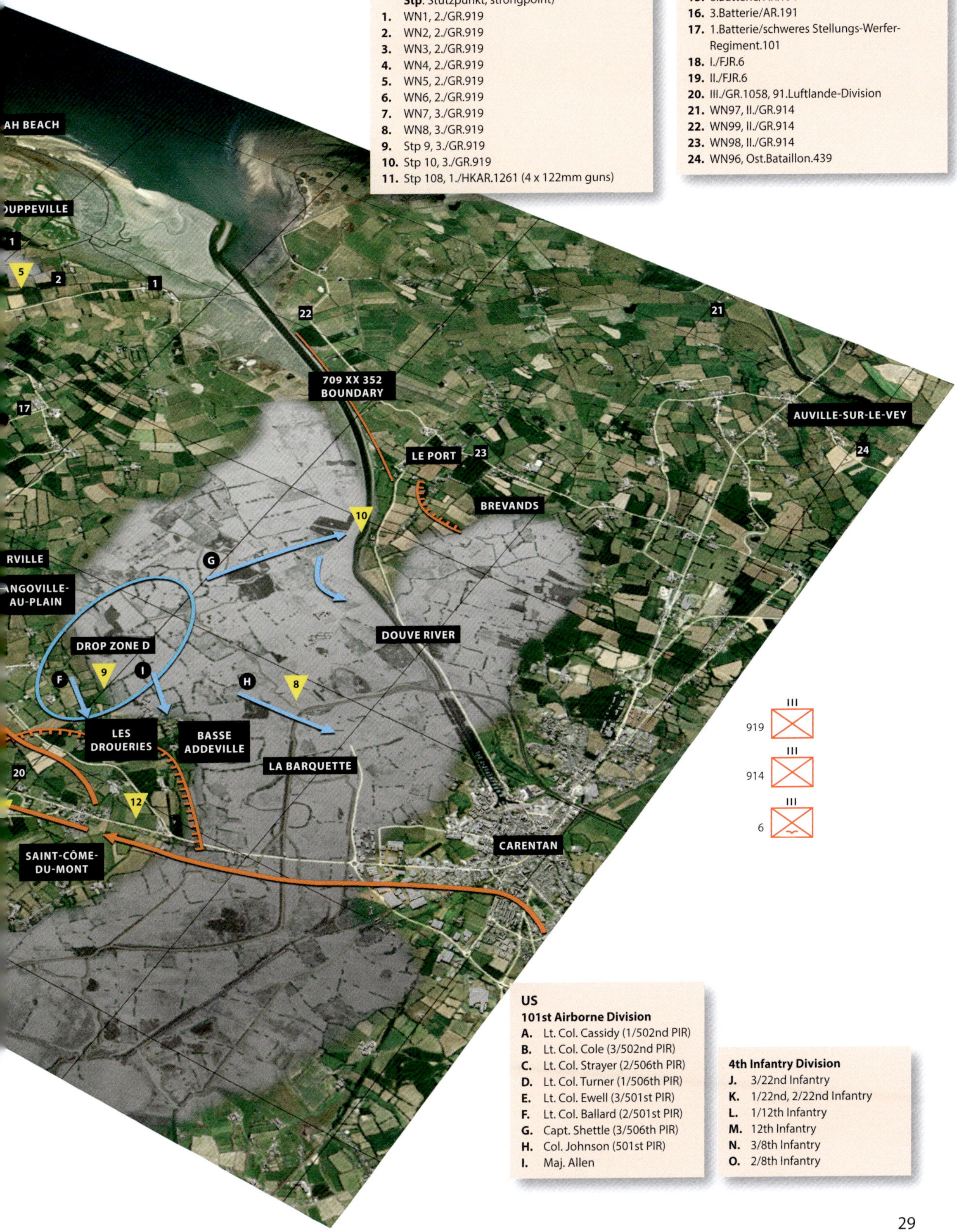

GERMAN UNITS AND FORTIFIED POSITIONS
(**WN**: Widerstandnest, platoon-sized defense work;
Stp: Stützpunkt, strongpoint)

1. WN1, 2./GR.919
2. WN2, 2./GR.919
3. WN3, 2./GR.919
4. WN4, 2./GR.919
5. WN5, 2./GR.919
6. WN6, 2./GR.919
7. WN7, 3./GR.919
8. WN8, 3./GR.919
9. Stp 9, 3./GR.919
10. Stp 10, 3./GR.919
11. Stp 108, 1./HKAR.1261 (4 x 122mm guns)
12. 14./GR.919
13. 13./GR.919
14. Georgisch-Bataillon.795
15. 6.Batterie/AR.191
16. 3.Batterie/AR.191
17. 1.Batterie/schweres Stellungs-Werfer-Regiment.101
18. I./FJR.6
19. II./FJR.6
20. III./GR.1058, 91.Luftlande-Division
21. WN97, II./GR.914
22. WN99, II./GR.914
23. WN98, II./GR.914
24. WN96, Ost.Bataillon.439

US

101st Airborne Division

A. Lt. Col. Cassidy (1/502nd PIR)
B. Lt. Col. Cole (3/502nd PIR)
C. Lt. Col. Strayer (2/506th PIR)
D. Lt. Col. Turner (1/506th PIR)
E. Lt. Col. Ewell (3/501st PIR)
F. Lt. Col. Ballard (2/501st PIR)
G. Capt. Shettle (3/506th PIR)
H. Col. Johnson (501st PIR)
I. Maj. Allen

4th Infantry Division

J. 3/22nd Infantry
K. 1/22nd, 2/22nd Infantry
L. 1/12th Infantry
M. 12th Infantry
N. 3/8th Infantry
O. 2/8th Infantry

for the outnumbered paratroopers to overcome the German defenders in house-to-house fighting.

Fighting flared up near the divisional command post in Drop Zone C due to a concentration of German troops around Sainte-Marie-du-Mont. The town itself was held by 1./GR.919 under Oberleutnant Gluba, reinforced by Abteilung Schmidt, a forward detachment of the 91.Luftlande-Division consisting of two 105mm howitzer batteries of Artillerie-Regiment.191 and a platoon of infantry from Grenadier-Regiment.1058. Paratroopers under Lt. Dick Winters of Co. E, 506th PIR assaulted the 6.Batterie/AR.191 near Brécourt Manor. This action has been immortalized in an episode of the popular TV series, *Band of Brothers*. The neighboring 3.Batterie/AR.191 near Férme Houelbec in Holdy was captured by a group of paratroopers under Capt. Lloyd Patch of HQ, 1/506th PIR, and Capt. Knut Raudstein of Co. C, 506th PIR. Winters, Patch, and Raudstein were all awarded the Distinguished Service Cross for their actions on D-Day.

The final groups to land were the 1/501st PIR, elements of the 2/501st PIR, the 3/506th PIR, as well as engineer and medical personnel. These forces were earmarked for Drop Zone D, the southernmost of the drop zones. The approach to the drop zone was hot, with a considerable amount of light flak, searchlights, and flares. Six C-47s were shot down and 26 damaged. These drops were among the most successful in putting the paratroopers near their intended objective. This was not entirely fortuitous, as the Germans had assumed that this area could be used for airborne landings, so they had troops near the landing-zone. Despite casualties, elements of 1/501st PIR under regimental commander Col. Howard Johnson set off for the primary objective, the La Barquette lock, which controlled the flooding of the areas along the Douve River, and captured it by early morning. Lt. Col. Robert Ballard's 2/501st PIR spent most of the day fighting around Les Droueries with elements of the III./GR.1058.

The third unit landing in Drop Zone D, the 3/506th PIR, had the roughest time. German troops were waiting in the landing area and had soaked a wooden building with fuel. They set the building on fire, illuminating the descending paratroopers. The battalion commander and his executive officer were among those killed in the first moments. Nonetheless, detachments

The three captains who led the attacks on the two artillery batteries of Abteilung Schmidt were (left to right) Capt. Lloyd Patch (HQ Co., 1/506th PIR), Capt. Knut Raudstein (Co. C, 506th PIR), and Capt. Richard Winters (Co. E, 506th PIR). All three were subsequently awarded the Distinguished Service Cross for their leadership on D-Day.

from the unit managed to fight their way free and seize the Douve River bridge at Le Port.

Overall, the 101st Airborne Division landed 6,885 troops on D-Day, of whom about 1,500 were killed, missing, or captured. About 1,100 paratroopers were on or near their intended drop zones at the start of the day. By the day's end, about 2,500 men, or about a third, were with organized groups capable of carrying out their assignments. Of the weapons and supply bundles airdropped on D-Day, only about 40 percent were collected by the paratroopers, leaving many units very low on ammunition. Of its specific missions, the destruction of the Saint-Martin-de-Varreville battery had been accomplished by air attack before the paratroopers had arrived. The La Barquette lock had been captured, but not the neighboring bridges. Even if all its specific objectives had not been attained, the overall mission had been successful. The disruption of their defenses by the surprise airborne landings had completely upset the Germans. The 4th Infantry Division landed with minimal casualties and proceeded to exit the beachhead area via the causeways without serious interference. The presence of large numbers of airborne detachments prevented the Germans from moving forces against Utah Beach.

Early on D-Day morning, paratroopers from the 101st Airborne Division captured this war-booty Renault UE armored tractor towing a war-booty French 47mm Pak 181(f) antitank gun in the Ravenoville area, along with these prisoners from Georgisch-Bataillon.795.

Pfc. Wilbur Shanklin of the HQ Co., 506th PIR, guards a prisoner from Georgisch-Bataillon.795 captured in Turqueville on D-Day. This was part of a series of photos staged by Signal Corps photographers.

The German D-Day response

The 101st Airborne Division drop zones contained a confusing assortment of German troops, as they were located along the southern seam of the German defenses. Elements of GR.919 of the 709.Infanterie-Division manned the coastal strongpoints, most of which were overrun by late morning by the US Army's 4th Infantry Division. There were scattered German units behind the beach, notably Georgisch.Bataillon.735 (Georgian Battalion 735) in the Turqueville area, and Major Diekhoff's III./GR.1058 from the 91.Luftlande-Division around Saint-Côme-du-Mont.

Around 2300hrs on the night of June 5, Major von der Heydte was warned by Luftwaffe radar stations in Cherbourg that an invasion was likely that night. The three battalions of FJR.6 were alerted around midnight, shortly after which reports began of Allied bombing raids along the coast. The first reports of paratroop landings came from I./FJR.6. Von der Heydte attempted to contact 84.AK headquarters and the 91.Luftlande-Division command post, but the commercial telephone lines were not functional, presumably cut by the French resistance.

The 84.AK headquarters in Saint-Lô had been receiving reports about the airborne landings from the 709.Infanterie-Division and

Numerous paratroopers were dropped away from their intended drop zones. These three members of the 377th Parachute Field Artillery Battalion were dropped near Cherbourg, and it took them 17 days to rejoin the 101st Airborne Division near Carentan.

91.Luftlande-Division via secure army communication lines from the early morning of June 6. General Marcks was concerned that the Allies would conduct additional airborne landings around Lessay on the western coast of the Cotentin peninsula, cutting off Cherbourg. As a result, he was hesitant to commit Fallschirmjäger-Regiment.6 until the situation was clarified. By dawn, it was becoming apparent that there were no airborne landings on the west Cotentin coast. Consequently, at 0600hrs, General Marcks contacted von der Heydte, ordering him to mobilize his regiment and move toward the coast. Von der Heydte's mission was to clear the Carentan area of American paratroopers as well as those in the area behind the 709.Infanterie-Division up to Sainte-Mère-Église. Marcks also authorized von der Heydte to take command of any units he found in the Saint-Côme-du-Mont area. Von der Heydte and his staff traveled to Carentan, where they found no American paratroopers, but also a very modest German presence.

Around 1100hrs, von der Heydte traveled to Saint-Côme-du-Mont by motorcycle. Climbing to the top of the church steeple, he had a view all the way to the coast and could clearly see the large Allied armada out to sea. He established a new regimental headquarters in a gully south of Saint-Côme-du-Mont. Recognizing his unit's lack of trucks, his instructions were based on the proximity of his three battalions to the battle-zone. Preikschat's I./FJR.6 was ordered to advance to Sainte-Marie-du-Mont to block the enemy advance off the beach. It was 22km from Raids to Sainte-Marie-du-Mont, so even at a good pace, it would take Preikschat's battalion at least seven hours to reach its objectives, even if not facing any resistance. Mager's II./FJR.6 was ordered to advance toward Saint-Côme-du-Mont and cover the left flank of I./FJR.6, a marching distance of over 30km. Since Trebes' III./FJR.6 was heavily engaged with paratroopers from the 101st Airborne Division who had been dropped south of Carentan, his battalion was ordered to advance to Carentan, clear up any American paratroopers in the area, and then proceed to Saint-Côme-du-Mont, acting as the rearguard of the regiment.

Traveling around Saint-Côme-du-Mont, von der Heydte located two artillery batteries of the 91.Luftlande-Division – the 4./ and 8./AR.191 – and put them under his command. The 4./AR.191 was assigned to support Preikschat's I./FJR.6, and the 8./AR.191 to Mager's II./FJR.6. He also located Major Diekhoff's III./GR.1058 of the 91.Luftlande-Division defending Saint-Côme-du-Mont and placed this unit under his command as well. Later in the day, 84.AK headquarters informed him that Ost-Bataillon.635 had been ordered to march to Carentan, reinforcing his force.

The lead elements of Preikschat's I./FJR.6 arrived near Saint-Côme-du-Mont in the afternoon and von der Heydte instructed them to continue to the northeast to Sainte-Marie-du-Mont to block any US troops exiting the beaches. Preikschat's battalion headed out of Saint-Côme-du-Mont after 1900hrs, and around 2100hrs passed by Angoville-au-Plain. Unexpectedly, the skies near the village were full of gliders. This was Mission *Keokuk*, a reinforcement consisting of 32 Horsa gliders arriving in Landing Zone L. Preikschat's troops fired on the gliders, and claimed to have captured "hundreds of prisoners." This claim is not supported by American accounts of the landings, which indicate only ten men missing or captured. With nightfall approaching, the I./FJR.6 halted for the night, still to the south of Sainte-Marie-du-Mont.

The 4./AR.191 had been providing fire support for the advance of Preikschat's battalion, but was spotted by a Shore Fire Support Party accompanying the 101st Airborne Division. The cruiser USS *Quincy* took the battery under fire with its 8in guns, killing 27 men of the artillery crews and forcing the battery to abandon its positions. Von der Heydte was unable to discover where it had escaped to until it was found the next day more than 10km away to the south of Carentan.

Mager's II./FJR.6 also advanced out of Saint-Côme-du-Mont around 1900hrs, oriented toward Hiesville. Its advance was disrupted by frequent encounters with US paratroopers, and at nightfall the battalion encamped in open fields.

By midnight, von der Heydte's headquarters near Saint-Côme-du-Mont was separated from both Preikschat's and Mager's battalions by American paratrooper patrols. The American advance "threw [Preikschat's] battalion into hopeless confusion," according to von der Heydte. Marcks' 84.AK headquarters informed von der Heydte that the corps' main mission on June 7 would be a pincer attack against Sainte-Mère-Église, with a Kampfgruppe based on GR.1058 attacking from the north, while his own command would form a Kampfgruppe attacking up the Saint-Côme-du-Mont–Sainte-Mère-Église road as the southern arm of the attack.

D+1: Advancing from the drop zones

On D-Day evening, Gen. Taylor traveled from the division command post in Hiesville to the 506th PIR headquarters in neighboring Culoville to deliberate with Col. Sink about the next day's mission. In view of the progress of the 4th Infantry Division advancing beyond the beachhead, the northern sector seemed secure. The 101st Airborne had not yet secured or destroyed the various Douve bridges, with some exceptions: Col. Johnson did hold the crossing at the La Barquette lock with some 150 men, and Capt. Charles Shettle had about 55 men from the 3/506th PIR at the two Douve bridges near Le Port.

In view of the chaotic situation on the division's southern front, Taylor decided that the principal D+1 mission would be to capture the town of

The landings left paratroopers from various units scattered outside their assigned drop-zone. This group in Ravenoville on D-Day under Maj. Stopka of the 502nd PIR included men from H/505th and A/506th PIR. The paratrooper holding the German flag is Pfc. James W. Flanagan from C/502nd PIR. The flag was displayed for many years at the Gen. Donald Pratt 101st Airborne Museum in Fort Campbell, Kentucky.

Saint-Côme-du-Mont as the first stage in securing the Douve River line. This mission was assigned to the 1/506th PIR under Lt. Col. William L. Turner and 2/506th PIR led by Lt. Col. Robert L. Strayer. These forces totaled about 525 paratroopers, plus another 100 men from miscellaneous units including a contingent from the 82nd Airborne who had been dropped too far east. The 1/410th GIR was also instructed to take part, but it did not arrive in time. The operation was to start at 0430hrs.

On the German side, the plan for von der Heydte's forces to take part in the attack on Sainte-Mère-Église on the morning of June 7 had become impossible. Before dawn, von der Heydte was able to reach Mager's battalion and he ordered them to withdraw to Saint-Côme-du-Mont and establish a semicircle around the town a kilometer to the east and 3km west of the town. He was unable to reach Preikschat's battalion by radio. After dawn, he sent a messenger to Preikschat, but this attempt failed. He then decided to use a more substantial team from the regiment's bicycle reconnaissance platoon. This patrol reached only about 500–800m from Saint-Côme-du-Mont when it was stopped by US paratroopers who were advancing down the same road. In view of the deteriorating situation, von der Heydte ordered Trebes' III.Bataillon to send two of its companies from the Carentan area to reinforce the regiment for the forthcoming day's actions.

Out of touch with von der Heydte, by dawn, Preikschat realized his battalion was becoming surrounded by US paratroopers and infantry formations pouring off Utah Beach, so he followed von der Heydte's initial instructions to withdraw to Saint-Côme-du-Mont if necessary. However, his battalion began withdrawing too late to avoid contact with the 101st Airborne Division, with deadly consequences.

As a result of this change of orders, the main German defense line from Hiesville to Les Droueries was held by Mager's II./FJR.6 on either side of the local D913 road, which would be the main focal point of the day's fighting. Further south, Major Diekhoff's III./GR.1058 was assigned the defense of the area immediately east of Saint-Côme-du-Mont, from the right wing of II./FJR.6 at Les Droueries to the hamlets of Basse Addeville and Belle Eneau. Von der Heydte's headquarters was near the junction of Route D913 and the main N13 national road from Saint-Côme-du-Mont to Carentan. Two companies of Trebes' III./FJR.6 were held in reserve, with another of the battalion's companies left in the Carentan area to deal with US paratroopers who had been dropped too far south.

Paratroopers of Co. H, 3/502nd PIR, 101st Airborne Division, march through the church square in Sainte-Marie-du-Mont on D+1, June 7, 1944.

At the start of the day's fighting, Turner's 1/506th PIR led the way from Culoville to Vierville on the D913, heading southwest. The paratroopers arrived in the village around 0900hrs, finding it largely empty of German troops. Gen. Taylor contacted Col. Sink by radio and instructed him to continue southward toward the hamlet of Beaumont, about 1,700 yards further down the road. Gen. Taylor walked down to Vierville shortly after and went up the church steeple with Col. Sink to survey the terrain. The area consisted of small farm fields edged in bocage, meaning that visibility from ground level was very limited. About 2,000 yards away to the southeast they spotted several hundred troops passing through the bocage toward Carentan. They could not identify the troops through binoculars, and since they were uncertain of the location of the 2/501st PIR, they decided against calling in artillery. A patrol was sent out and discovered they were indeed Germans. By the time the patrol returned to Vierville, the Germans were beyond view. This mystery group was most of Preikschat's I./FJR.6.

A half-dozen M4 tanks of Co. A, 746th Tank Battalion under Capt. Loueaire Hedges arrived to reinforce the paratroopers. The 2/A/746th Tank Battalion was assigned to Ballard's 2/501st PIR in the Les Droueries area east of the main group, while 3/A/746th Tank Battalion was assigned to support the 1st and 2nd Battalions of the 506th PIR on the advance from Vierville to Beaumont.

After the 1/506th PIR passed through Vierville, it was followed in column by the 2/506th PIR. A company from Preikschat's I./FJR.6 had become isolated on the west side of the D913 road. Seeing a gap in the paratrooper columns, they attempted to infiltrate to the east side. However, they ran into American paratroopers from Strayer's 2/506th PIR, starting a significant firefight inside the village. In the midst of this, the tanks from the 746th Tank Battalion arrived, joining the melee. Leutnant Scherer's 4.Kompanie had a 75mm Pak 40 antitank gun and some Panzerschreck rocket launchers, and managed to knock out three M4 tanks, including Hedges' command tank. After about an hour-and-a-half of fighting, German resistance in the village was subdued, with an estimated 150 Fallschirmjäger being killed and about 140 captured.

The terrain east of Saint-Côme-du-Mont was fragmented by bocage. This is Les Droueries, where Ballard's 2/501st PIR fought against III./GR.1058. The D913 road is on the left, while the village of Beaumont is in the upper center.

Advance to Saint-Côme-du-Mont, D+1 (June 7)

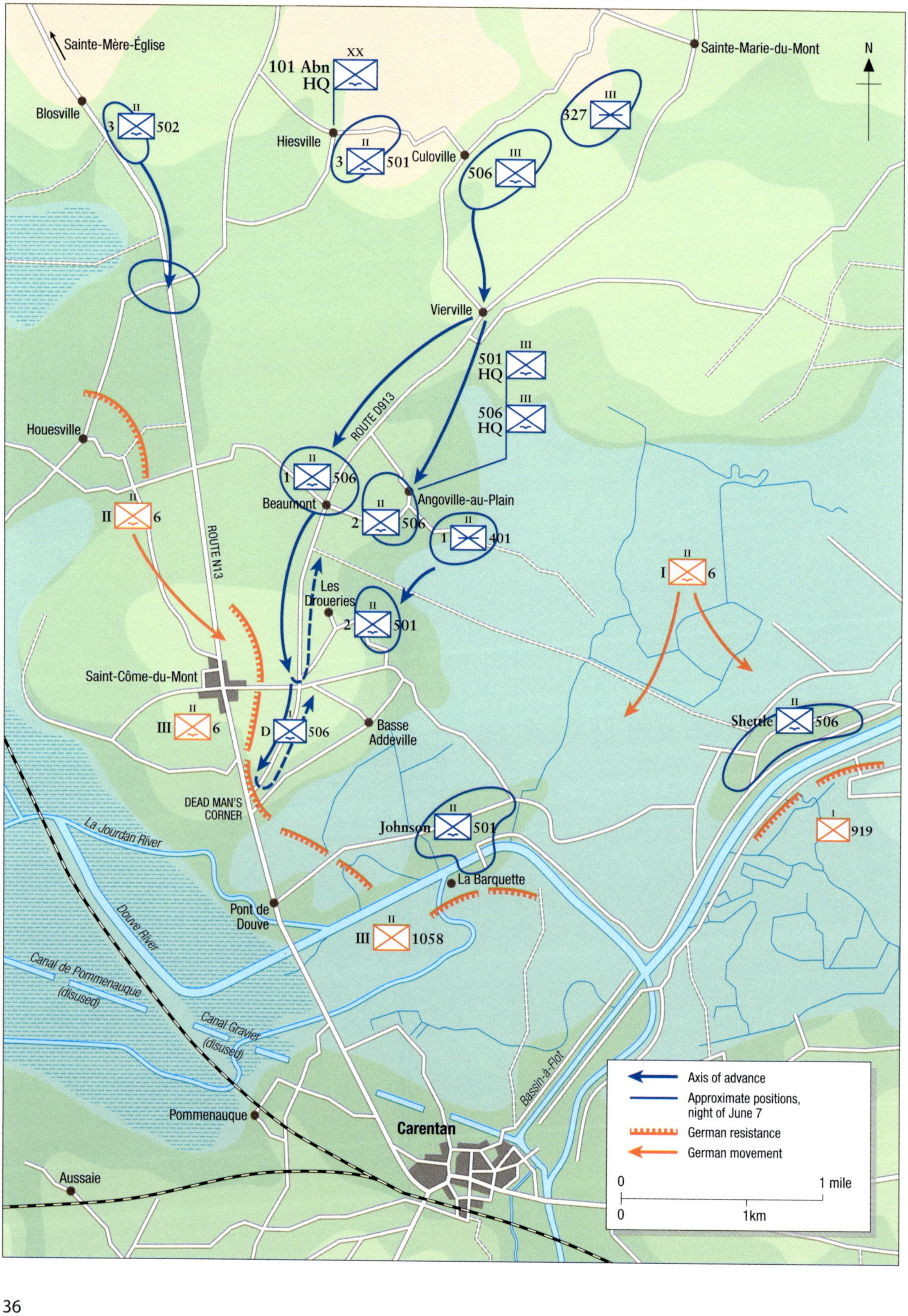

Turner's 1/506th PIR continued down the main road toward Beaumont while Strayer's 2/506th PIR went eastward, reaching the village of Angoville-au-Plain around 1100hrs. Turner's 1/506th PIR reached Beaumont at 1130hrs and became heavily engaged against Mager's II./FJR.6, which had established strong defensive positions in the hedgerows as well as in a farm immediately west of the D913 road. The paratroopers managed to push into the farm at least twice, only to be forced back out again by determined Fallschirmjäger attacks. Turner directed the M4 medium tanks of the 746th Tank Battalion forward, but the lead tank was hit twice by rocket fire and retreated to Beaumont. Turner climbed on the lead tank to direct the fire. As the tank approached the German defenses, Turner raised his head out of the hatch to get a better view and was killed by rifle fire. Turner's death in front of his troops had a demoralizing effect, and the fighting near Beaumont became a stalemate. Around 1600hrs, the tank platoon returned to Angoville-au-Plain to refuel and get more ammunition. Sink reinforced the Beaumont attack with Capt. Jerre Gross' Co. D, which had 94 men at the time, making it the strongest company in the division.

Co. A, 746th Tank Battalion, was assigned to support the 101st Airborne Division during the fighting east of Saint-Côme-du-Mont. This is "Apache," an M4 dozer tank of the unit.

The reinforcements from Co. D helped provide the necessary momentum, and the Fallschirmjäger defenses in the farm were finally overcome. The 1/506th PIR continued down the road through Beaumont, aiming for the junction of the D913 and the main N13 road from Saint-Côme-du-Mont to Carentan. By this time, the tank support was being provided by three M5A1 light tanks of Co. D, 70th Tank Battalion. In the gathering dusk, the M5A1s led the way, spraying the hedgerows along the road with machine-gun fire. They reached the crossroads around 2300hrs and fired orange flares to inform the rest of the battalion that they had arrived at the objective. Shortly after the flares were fired, German troops on either side of the road opened fire on Co. D. The lead M5A1 tank, No. 12 "Delphia," commanded by Sgt. Anthony Tomasheski, was hit and knocked out by a Panzerfaust fired by Obergefreiter Fischer of II./FJR.6. This tank sat at the intersection for several days with its dead crewmen, leading to the location's grim nickname, "Dead Man's Corner."

The units behind Co. D, including Cos. B and C, received verbal instructions to withdraw to Beaumont. The source of these orders remains confused. Col. Sink, realizing that Co. D was now left exposed at the crossroads, ordered it to pull back to Beaumont. They did so reluctantly, not wishing to waste their effort and feeling they could hold the position. Sink informed them that Taylor had decided to consolidate his forces for a final assault on Saint-Côme-du-Mont the following morning.

D+1: Hell's Corner

While the two battalions of the 506th PIR were fighting down the Vierville–Beaumont road, isolated paratrooper elements were engaged further to the southeast along the waterways leading to Carentan. Capt. Charles Shettle had about 75 men from the 3/506th PIR at the two Douve bridges near Le Port on the outskirts of Carentan. Facing a company of German infantry on the opposite bank, his force gradually increased to about 135 men. Shettle contacted Col. Johnson's force at the La Barquette lock on D-Day, but Johnson's positions were too weak to offer them much assistance. Around noon on June 7, Shettle's detachment spotted a patrol of fighters, variously described as P-51s or P-47s, and used signal panels to request an attack on German positions on the opposite bank of the Douve.

By the afternoon, Col. Sink was concerned that the two Douve bridges had not been destroyed and so placed a request for an air strike. The 353rd Fighter Group was assigned the mission and dispatched a sortie that arrived over the Douve around 1430hrs. They dropped a dozen bombs, hitting both bridges, but at least three bombs landed within the paratrooper positions.

Around 1530hrs, Shettle's force was approached from the rear by about 300 Germans trying to reach the Douve River to cross over to Carentan. These appear to have been from Preikschat's I./FJR.6 and Gluba's 1./GR.919. Shettle's men prepared an ambush. Once the Germans had approached, Shettle's force opened fire, killing 60–70 enemy. This was followed by the surrender of the remaining 258 Germans. These Germans did not resist as vigorously as another group further to the west that bumped into Col. Johnson's force at the La Barquette lock. This was probably because Preikschat and most of the senior officers were with the main body to the west.

Early on D-Day, Col. Howard Johnson of the 501st PIR had about 150 men at the Douve lock at La Barquette. Later in the day, they made contact with a group of another 100 paratroopers led by the regimental S-3, Maj. R.J. Allen, eventually joining their forces together. They tried to merge with Lt. Col. Robert Ballard's force of 250 men from the 2/501st PIR in Les Droueries further to the west, but Ballard was so heavily engaged with III./GR.1058 that this proved impossible. Fortunately for Johnson, his force included Lt. Farrell from one of the Shore Fire Support Parties assigned to the division. Late on the night of D-Day, he contacted USS *Quincy* offshore to bombard a German field artillery battery east of Carentan that was firing on the locks. Farrell also requested strikes on the bridges leading from Saint-Côme-du-Mont to Carentan, but failed to bring them down.

On D+1, Johnson again contacted Ballard in Les Droueries and asked that he merge his force with his detachment at the locks. Ballard contacted the divisional headquarters, who told him to continue his fight against the German defenses in the sector. In the early afternoon, the 506th PIR sent a platoon of M4 medium tanks from A/746th Tank Battalion to assist. Ballard described their contribution of firepower as "like rainfall in the desert," helping to overcome the III./GR.1058 defenses.

In the afternoon, a forward observation post on the eastern side of Ballard's detachment spotted Preikschat's battalion advancing toward the Douve River about 200–600 yards away. They substantially outnumbered Ballard's force, so there was some reluctance to engage them for fear of having them emerge from the swamp and overrun their positions. Most of the Fallschirmjäger continued their escape to the southeast, but a group

of about 20 bumped into the left side of Ballard's detachment. About a dozen were killed and the remainder surrendered.

Meanwhile, on the morning of D+1, Johnson's 501st PIR detachment at the La Barquette lock had little contact with the Germans except for persistent mortar and artillery fire. Their main problem was a severe shortage of ammunition. Around 0630hrs on D+1, an air supply mission was flown but the bundles fell into the marshes east of Angoville-au-Plain. Attempts to retrieve them failed, as they were in sight of the III./GR.1058 positions near Basse Addeville.

By mid-afternoon, the main body of Preikschat's I./FJR.6 was heading toward the locks to escape over the Douve. By 1500hrs, they were traversing the marshes north of Johnson's position, around the same time that the other group encountered Shettle's force near the Douve bridges. The Fallschirmjäger failed to deploy scouts in front of their advance, perhaps believing that no American troops were this far south. In the event, Johnson's men spotted the Fallschirmjäger first. Six .30 cal machine guns were moved up to the northeast perimeter along with the detachment's three 60mm mortars. As many troops as possible were shifted there as well, leaving only a minimal force elsewhere. Johnson's force took about a half-hour to prepare their ambush. According to his later account, Johnson's intention was "to achieve a delicate balance in firepower – to lead the enemy up to the point where the first volley would sweep them with a killing blast and yet not permit them to come so close that they could come on and overwhelm the position by sheer weight of numbers." By rough estimate, over 600 Fallschirmjäger were facing about 250 US paratroopers.

Around 1600hrs, the Fallschirmjäger had advanced to within about 350 yards from the American ambush when Johnson yelled, "OK now – Let 'em have it!" The initial wave of fire killed numerous Germans, but the remainder used the reeds and irregular ground in the marsh to take cover.

This aerial photo taken in 1947 shows the La Barquette lock on the Douve to the lower left. The battle of "Hell's Corner" took place in fields to the upper right that were flooded in 1944. (AHEC)

German observers from the III./GR.1058 nearby in Basse Addeville attempted to intervene by calling in artillery fire from Carentan and mortar fire from Saint-Côme-du-Mont on Johnson's positions.

After about a half-hour of gunfire, with Johnson's men running low on ammunition, he decided to try to get the trapped Germans to surrender. His men objected, saying they preferred to keep firing until they wiped out the German detachment. Regardless, Johnson and two volunteers stood up with an orange flag tied to a rifle. There was still sporadic rifle fire from the American lines, so they found a longer pole to mount the flag. Johnson and his party advanced about 100 yards and a few Germans emerged. After closing the distance by 25 yards, the Germans ducked for cover and the German line erupted in rifle fire. Johnson was hit in the hand and one of his men in the arm. They crawled back to their lines.

The firefight continued for another half-hour until the volume of fire from the German side markedly decreased. Assuming the Germans were running out of ammunition, Johnson and the two paratroopers again tried to conduct another parley. Two wounded German soldiers then moved forward. They said that most of the men wanted to surrender but the officers and NCOs refused and had already shot a few soldiers who had earlier tried to surrender. Johnson sent one of his men back to collect a white tablecloth, which he gave to one of the Germans. He instructed them to return to their lines, and when they were ready to surrender, to come forward without helmets and weapons, waving the tablecloth.

Firing resumed, but the fire from the German side was increasingly spotty. After another half-hour, a group of Germans emerged and began to walk forward. As they were coming toward the American lines, a single rifle began firing from the American side. Johnson turned around to see a young lieutenant firing. Johnson shouted at him, "God damn it! What are you doing!" The lieutenant replied: "God damn it, colonel. Those bastards have been killing my men all day and now you won't let me shoot them." According to Johnson, the exhausted lieutenant then broke down, crying like a child. Johnson ordered him back to the command post to avoid any further incidents.

Once the firing had died down again, the Germans began walking out of the marshes under the white surrender flag, reaching the perimeter around 1800hrs. The surrender began as small groups and continued until nightfall.

The fighting on D+1 took place in the fields east of Saint-Côme-du-Mont seen here. The town, as its name implies, was located on elevated ground. The steeple of the town's 12th-century church, Saint-Côme-et-Saint-Damien, can be seen on the horizon to the right. (AHEC)

Preikschat was the last to arrive. He told Johnson that he had a right to parley and to decide whether to surrender or not. Johnson had no patience and shoved him into line with the other prisoners. There were about 350 German prisoners and Johnson estimated that there were 150 dead or severely wounded still in the marshes. German accounts indicate that only about two dozen Fallschirmjäger from Preikschat's I./FJR.6 managed to escape. US losses were ten killed and 30 wounded.

The German prisoners outnumbered Johnson's detachment, so he planned to confine them in a farm building in Peneme on the southwestern end of the American perimeter. While the German prisoners were lined up on the road, a salvo of German artillery from Carentan fell onto the road, killing 20 Germans as well as Capt. Altus McReynolds, the regimental adjutant, and wounding several American officers at the nearby command post. Preikschat was probably among those killed, as there is no further mention of him. The night was spent retrieving wounded Fallschirmjäger from the swamp.

The 65th Armored Field Artillery Battalion, equipped with the M7 105mm howitzer motor carriage, provided fire support for the 101st Airborne Division's drive from Utah Beach to Saint-Côme-du-Mont. This is one of the self-propelled howitzers of Battery A.

Johnson's detachment remained on guard at "Hell's Corner" through D+2 without as much action, the focus that day being on the battle for Saint-Côme-du-Mont. By the end of D+1, the 101st Airborne had captured 755 German troops, most of them in these three incidents along the Douve River.

D+2: The battle for Saint-Côme-du-Mont

By nightfall of D+1, Gen. Taylor considered that German defenses around Saint-Côme-du-Mont remained the main barrier to reaching Carentan. Over the course of D+1, the US paratrooper forces east of Saint-Côme-du-Mont had significantly increased in size and strength. Taylor assigned Col. Sink the mission of capturing the village on D+2. He was allotted elements of five battalions, including 1/ and 2/506th PIR, 2/ and 3/501st PIR, and 1/401st GIR. He also had eight tanks attached, five 57mm antitank guns, and five 37mm antitank guns. Artillery support was provided by the 65th Armored Field Artillery Battalion with 18 M7 105mm howitzer motor carriages, as well as one 75mm howitzer and one German 105mm field howitzer captured at Holdy. The US plan was to lead with the fresh 1/401st GIR, which would form the left wing of the assault, passing through Ballard's exhausted 2/501st PIR to seal off the Saint-Côme-du-Mont–Carentan road south of Dead Man's Corner. Three other companies would advance on their right, sealing off the

Paratroopers advance outside Saint-Côme-du-Mont through a field covered with the bodies of paratroopers and Fallschirmjäger killed during the earlier fighting.

GRAHAM TURNER

GERMAN DEFENSE OF SAINT-CÔME-DU-MONT, JUNE 8, 1944 (PP.42–43)

The determined defense of Saint-Côme-du-Mont by von der Heydte's Fallschirmjäger-Regiment.6 delayed the advance of the 101st Airborne Division to Carentan. This illustration shows a team from 12.Kompanie of the III./FJR.6 setting up a defensive position on the edge of town. The 12.Kompanie was the heavy company of the III.Bataillon and so had many of the battalion's fire support weapons. In the foreground is an MG42 heavy machine-gun team. The MG42 was deployed in two principal forms: as a light machine gun, equipped with a forward bipod, and as a heavy machine gun **(1)**, deployed with a tripod mount, the Lafette 42. The tripod had adjustable legs to set its height and is shown here in the depressed position, allowing the crew to fire from a prone position. The tripod was fitted with a telescopic sight **(2)**, allowing the crew to engage targets as far as 3,000m away. It offered a steadier platform for the machine gun than the bipod, permitting longer bursts of 20–30 rounds. A second crew can be seen behind, bringing up another MG42. German infantry tactics tended to revolve around their machine guns, a lesson from World War I.

Antitank rocket weapons began to appear in Normandy in June 1944, as seen with the two figures in the back. The kneeling figure is armed with a Panzerfaust 60 **(3)**, a disposable, one-shot, antitank grenade launcher. These had a very limited range, but were cheap to manufacture. They were issued as a munition, so there was no specific allotment for a company. In Normandy, in early June, they were still uncommon. Perhaps the most famous instance of their use in this battle was knocking out an M5A1 light tank at Dead Man's Corner south of Saint-Côme-du-Mont. The 88mm Panzerschreck **(4)** was a crew-served weapon, firing a rocket-propelled antitank munition. It was substantially larger and heavier than the Panzerfaust, but offered better range, about 150m as opposed to 60m. The Panzerschreck gunner was accompanied by a loader **(5)**, who also carried additional rockets in wooden boxes.

Saint-Côme-du-Mont–Carentan road on the eastern side. The remainder of the force would advance through Beaumont and into Saint-Côme-du-Mont.

Due to the heavy losses suffered by Mager's II./FJR.6 the previous day, von der Heydte moved up two companies – the 9. and 10. – from Trebes' III./FJR.6 as the main force, centered around his command post near Dead Man's Corner. The 13.Kompanie had its mortars set up behind a hill south of Dead Man's Corner. The remnants of III./GR.1058 were still holding the southern perimeter near Basse Addeville.

German engineers of Pionier-Bataillon.91 prematurely blew up the Douve railway bridge, complicating the withdrawal of II./FJR.6 from Saint-Côme-du-Mont to Carentan. This obstruction also forced the 101st Airborne Division to use the road causeway into Carentan instead of the railway causeway.

The American attack began around 0445hrs with an artillery preparation. This included a heavy dose of white phosphorous smoke rounds, which disrupted the German defenses since the smoke was toxic and the Fallschirmjäger were unprepared for its use. The paratroopers began advancing behind the barrage. Lt. Col. Julian Ewell's 3/501st PIR pushed through Les Droueries, facing little resistance from the battered III./GR.1058, which had already largely withdrawn westward in response to the artillery barrage earlier in the morning. The fighting was fairly confused as the terrain east of Saint-Côme-du-Mont was broken up by bocage and marshland. Co. H, 506th PIR was the first unit to enter the village around 0800hrs and ran into immediate resistance from Mager's depleted II./FJR.6.

Von der Heydte threw in his last reserves, including the bicycle scout section. Nevertheless, German troops began retreating out of the village around 1015hrs along the Saint-Côme-du-Mont–Carentan causeway, followed by troops from II./FJR.6 along the railway tracks.

Ewell's 3/501st reached the N13 highway north of Dead Man's Corner around 0800hrs and were immediately hit by a counterattack from the north, probably from the FJR.6 bicycle platoon and regimental Kampfzug as well as elements of II./FJR.6. The Fallschirmjäger concentrations located on the southern side of Saint-Côme-du-Mont hit Ewell's battalion six times between 0930hrs and 1600hrs, at one point pushing them back to the east side of the road. Two of the best Fallschirmjäger company commanders died in these attacks, Oberleutnant Helmuth Wagner of 9.Kompanie and Oberleutnant Pfiebe of 10.Kompanie. A critical moment came around 1430hrs when German fire seemed on the verge of pushing back the paratrooper advance. Ewell took immediate action, yelling

A Fallschirmjäger with an FG42 assault rifle during the fighting in the bocage in June 1944.

Capture of Saint-Côme-du-Mont, D+2 (June 8)

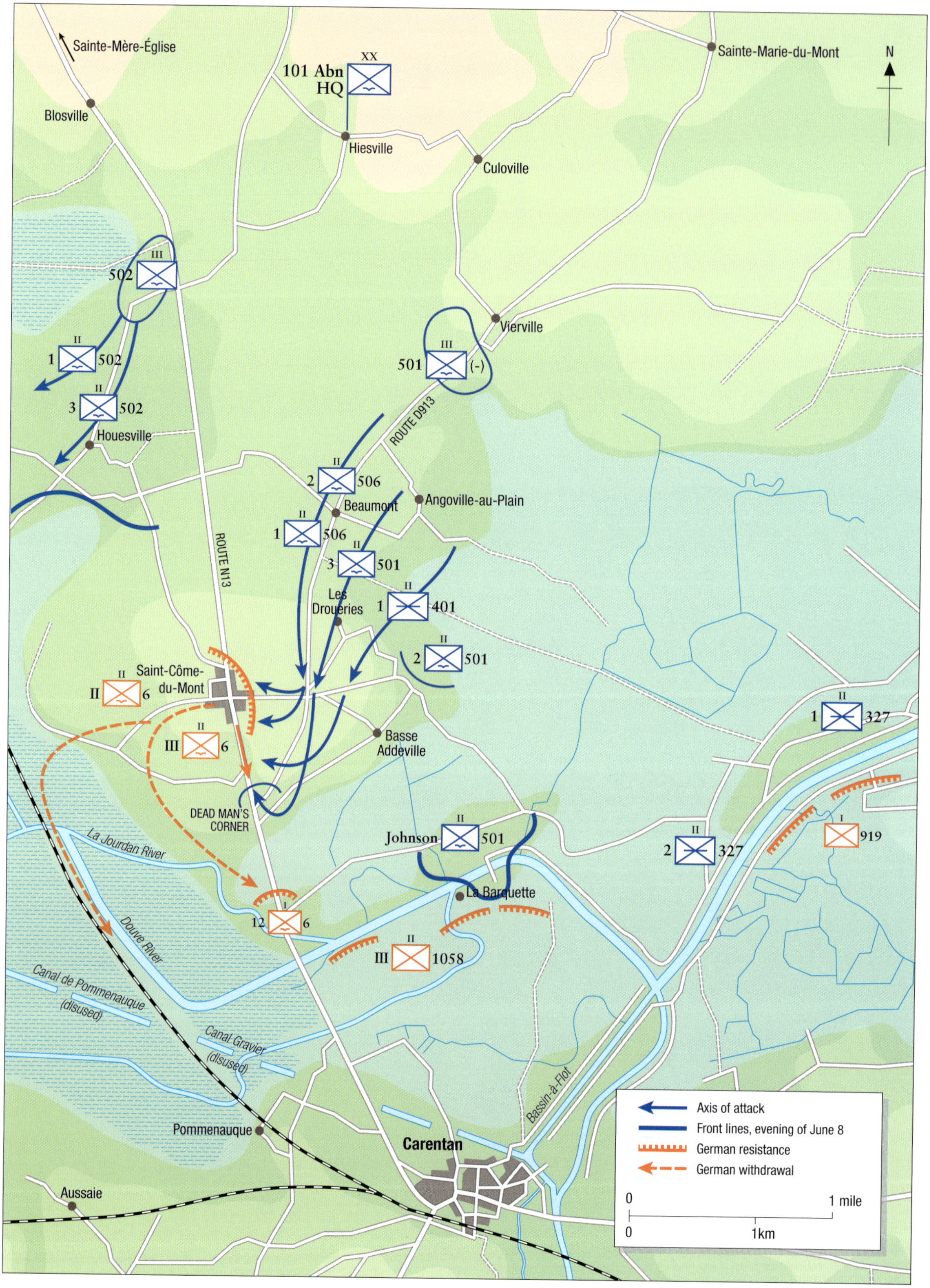

"Follow me" and crossing a hedgerow to hit the Germans' exposed flank. Ewell's charge coincided with the appearance of three M5A1 light tanks that bolstered the attack. Hard-pressed, Ewell headed back to locate reinforcements. He found that 1/401st GIR had still not advanced as planned across the N13 further south of his position, and finally got the men moving forward. Ewell's detachment lost 40 of its 160 men during the day's fighting, the heaviest casualties among the 101st Airborne Division units that participated that day.

Paratroopers, possibly from the 506th PIR, advance toward Carentan using an M3A4 airborne cart to help move ammunition and supplies.

By late afternoon, German troops were withdrawing out of Saint-Côme-du-Mont. Von der Heydte attempted to contact Mager's II./FJR.6, but was unable to do so. Mager, on his own initiative, had decided to withdraw his unit by moving through the marshes along the railway embankment. In the process, the unit lost most of its radio equipment as well as heavy weapons, as it had to swim across several flooded areas. Pionier-Bataillon.91 had rigged several of the Douve bridges for demolition, with the understanding that they would not be blown until authorized by von der Heydte. Regardless of these instructions, around 1400hrs, one of the road bridges on the Saint-Côme-du-Mont–Carentan causeway was demolished. In addition, one of the bridges on the railway line was also knocked down, though the timing of this incident is unclear. The unexpected demolition of the Douve bridges precipitated von der Heydte's decision to withdraw from Saint-Côme-du-Mont to Carentan. He was well aware that the area between the two towns was flooded, with the only exit routes being the elevated railway line and the N13 road causeway. With these routes interrupted by demolished bridges, his men would face considerable difficulty retreating to Carentan.

M5A1 D-12, named "Delphia," of Co. D, 70th Tank Battalion, was knocked out by a Panzerfaust hit on the hull side near the driver's station during the fighting near Saint-Côme-du-Mont. The wreck remained there for several days, leading to the grim nickname "Dead Man's Corner" for the road intersection.

The 12.Kompanie under the command of Oberfeldwebel Rentsch established a pair of rearguard machine-gun defenses on the approaches to the causeway near Pont de Douve. Von der Heydte, along with the III./FJR.6 and some elements of Diekhoff's III./GR.1058, withdrew down the N13 road causeway, swimming over the Douve where Bridge No. 2 had been dropped. The precipitate retreat from Saint-Côme-du-Mont and the bridge destruction resulted in the loss of the regiment's horse-drawn baggage train, with about 40 wagons being left behind. Most of the FJR.6 reached the eastern bank of the Douve River by 1700hrs, though stragglers continued to trickle in over the next day. The 8./AR.191 had already been withdrawn to Carentan on June 7, so was one of the few remaining sources of fire support.

THE BATTLE FOR CARENTAN

The defense of Carentan

The remnants of FJR.6 arrived in Carentan on the evening of D+2, June 8. By this time, the I./FJR.6 had been almost entirely destroyed. Mager's II./FJR.6 had suffered heavy casualties too and had lost nearly all of its heavy weapons. Trebes' III./FJR.6 was in the best shape of the three battalions, since one of its companies had remained behind in Carentan during the Saint-Côme-du-Mont fighting, and its other companies had been engaged only during the June 8 fighting.

Von der Heydte had an assortment of other forces at his disposal. Ost-Bataillon.635 had finally arrived on the east side of Carentan, but von der Heydte was skeptical of their combat value. Major Diekhoff's III./GR.1058, meanwhile, had suffered very heavy losses. There are few sources giving any precise figures, but it was probably in the low hundreds of men. There was also an assortment of personnel from the 709.Infanterie-Division who had been pushed back from Utah Beach. Some units that had been east of

A machine-gun team from FJR.6 inside Carentan during the fighting for the town. The lead Fallschirmjäger is armed with an MP40 machine pistol, while the soldier behind him is carrying a box of 7.92mm machine-gun ammunition.

The Lions of Carentan. From left to right: Hauptmann Emil Preikschat (I./FJR.6), Hauptmann Rolf Mager (II./FJR.6), and Hauptmann Horst Trebes (III./FJR.6). Mager and Trebes were both awarded the Knight's Cross for their leadership in the Carentan fighting.

Carentan joined KG Heydte, including II./GR.914 from the 352.Infanterie-Division and Major Hanns Becker's Ost-Bataillon.439. Fire support came mainly from 8./AR.191, which had been spared from the heaviest fighting in Saint-Côme-du-Mont. However, their exotic mountain howitzers were on the verge of running out of their specialized ammunition. The wandering 4./AR.191 was finally tracked down to the Baupte area and moved into the Carentan sector, though with little ammunition. There was also 3./Pz.Jg. Abt.243 with a few 20mm flak guns.

When the FJR.6 retreated into Carentan, von der Heydte first dispatched the remnants of Mager's II./FJR.6 to the road east of Carentan, having received alarming reports that advance patrols of the US Army were approaching from the Omaha Beach area. This proved to be false, and there was considerable shuffling of units over the next day as von der Heydte began to reassess the myriad threats encircling Carentan.

He reconfigured his initial dispositions. The 10. and 11.Kompanien of Trebes' III.Bataillon were deployed in the Pommenauque area facing the Saint-Côme-du-Mont–Carentan causeway, along with the machine-gun detachments established there by Oberfeldwebel Rentsch of 12.Kompanie from the fighting in Saint-Côme-du-Mont. Mager's II.Bataillon was committed to the sector from Pommenauque across the northern side of Carentan, defending against an attack from the north. Von der Heydte kept several platoons in reserve on the southern side of Carentan to deal with contingencies.

The heavy companies of both II. and III./FJR.6 were put under Oberleutnant Heinrich Graf von Benthusy-Huc, the leader of 8.Kompanie, and deployed on Hill 30 on the south side of Carentan. They were all eventually subsumed under Artillerie-Gruppe Rock, which included the 4./ and 8./AR.191 and 3./Flak.243. Their most persistent problem was the dwindling supply of ammunition.

Stragglers from the 709.Infanterie-Division in the Le Port area were withdrawn closer to the town too because they were too weak to resist any serious attack. There were also a variety of stragglers from the Isigny area who ended up on the eastern side of Carentan, and these were formed into small detachments. Most of the detachments facing eastward were put under the command of Major Hanns Becker of Ost-Bataillon.439.

One of von der Heydte's growing problems was a shortage of small-arms ammunition, most of the regiment's supplies having been left behind in the baggage train in Saint-Côme-du-Mont. The AOK.7 informed FJR.6 of several ammunition depots in the area, but one was found to be empty, another had been obliterated in an Allied raid, and a third was inaccessible due to downed bridges. The ammunition shortage thus persisted into the next day's fighting.

Command decisions

On D+3, June 9, Lt. Gen. Omar Bradley, commander of First US Army, visited Maj. Gen. J. Lawton Collins, the VII Corps commander, at his command post in Audouville. Until that point, the priority for VII Corps had been to push north from Utah Beach and capture the port of Cherbourg. By this time, however, Eisenhower had expressed his concern to Bradley that the juncture of Utah and Omaha Beaches had not occurred. There had been a steady stream of Ultra decryptions of German Enigma radio traffic reporting on the mobilization and transfer of Panzer divisions to the Normandy front. Eisenhower was concerned that the Germans could exploit the failure to connect the bridgeheads by staging a counterattack around Carentan.

A study of the area by SHAEF (Supreme Headquarters Allied Expeditionary Force) in London recommended an advance over the Carentan canal near Brevands, encircling Carentan from the north and east and joining the VII Corps and V Corps somewhere along the Vire River. Although Collins gave Gen. Taylor the mission to capture Carentan, he gave him some freedom on choosing the tactics. The area suggested by SHAEF was flooded and the approaches were interrupted by numerous rivers and a large river basin used as a port on the north side of the town. On June 8, an engineer reconnaissance party concluded that an advance along the Saint-Côme-du-Mont–Carentan causeway might be a better approach. The neighboring railway bridge was a less attractive option, the area having been much more thoroughly flooded.

On D+4, June 9, Col. Sink made a personal reconnaissance of the causeway. Bridge No. 1 over an extension of the Douve called La Jourdan was in American hands and presented no problem. Bridge No. 2 over the Douve had been blown up by the Germans. The river was about 25–30 yards wide at this point, but Sink and his party found a small boat and were able to cross

To replace the two wooden bridges over the Douve near Le Port destroyed by fighter-bombers on June 7, the 991st Engineer Treadway Bridge Company erected a treadway bridge on pontoons, as seen here in a pencil sketch by one of the engineers. This was used by the 327th GIR to cross the Douve during its advance on Carentan.

to the far side. They continued down the causeway to Bridge No. 3 over La Groult stream, where they encountered machine-gun fire. They halted before trying to reach Bridge No. 4, which crossed La Madeleine stream into the hamlet of Pommenauque on the western outskirts of Carentan. The divisional G-2 believed that after the losses in Saint-Côme-du-Mont, the German defenders were only a battalion in strength. Sink's report to the 502nd PIR was garbled and led the acting commander, Lt. Col. John H. Michaelis, to believe that Carentan was lightly held. That afternoon, Lt. Ralph Gehauf, the S-2 (intelligence) of the 3/502nd PIR, flew a reconnaissance mission over the causeway in an L-4 observation aircraft. Nevertheless, he learned little about German dispositions in Carentan, reinforcing the idea that the town was lightly held. Late on June 9, Capt. Henry Plitt, regimental S-3, flew another flight over the railway bridge to determine whether it was passable as an alternate route. He discovered that a 10-yard, elevated section of the bridge had been knocked down, making it impossible as an alternative passage. He flew around Carentan at dusk, drawing no fire from the German troops, further reinforcing the mistaken belief that the town was lightly held. The 326th Airborne Engineer Battalion was assigned to bridge the gap on Bridge No. 2 after dark on the night of June 9/10.

The obvious problem of using the causeway for advancing into Carentan was that it was an entirely straight road, elevated 6–9ft over the marshes, and completely exposed to enemy fire on both sides. The distance from Bridge No. 1 to Bridge No. 4 was 775m, or about half a mile. There was no cover on the causeway except for occasional clumps of stunted poplar trees with little or no foliage.

Despite the risks of crossing the causeway, Taylor's plan was for the 502nd PIR to cross in column, with Lt. Col. Robert Cole's 3/502nd PIR in the lead. Their objective was Hill 30, immediately south of Carentan near the town's railroad station, which controlled the main road south to Périers. At the

The 327th GIR approached Carentan from the north, an area dominated by its waterways. The center feature is the Bassin-à-Flot, while the Douve River is to the right and the Canal de Vire et Taute on the left. This photo was taken in 1947 and many of the dry fields seen here were inundated in 1944. (AHEC)

same time, the 327th GIR was to cross the Carentan Canal and swing wide around the northern side of Carentan to avoid the marshes and flooded areas, bringing them into the town from the northeast. In the V Corps sector, the 29th Division was assigned to reach La Billonnerie to the west of Carentan.

Northern approaches

The 327th/401st GIR had begun preparations for crossing the Douve north of Carentan on the night of June 8/9. Around 1000hrs on June 9, a patrol swam across the river, later bolstered by more men using a small ferry. The scouting party ran into German defenses and was forced to retreat during the afternoon under fire. Preparations for a nighttime crossing were well underway, with rubber boats brought to the edge of the river. Around midnight on June 9/10, divisional artillery – including the 65th Armored FAB (Field Artillery Battalion) – conducted a preliminary bombardment of German positions while 1/327th GIR crossed the river. The river crossing faced light resistance. Once on the eastern bank, explosions rocked Co. C, causing several dozen casualties. Although this was attributed to German mines, there was some suspicion that it was in fact due to friendly artillery fire. Gen. Taylor was disturbed enough about the performance of the 327th GIR to date that he relieved Col. George S. Wear of command, replacing him with Col. Joseph H. Harper shortly after noon on June 10.

Once the 1st Battalion had crossed, the 49th Engineer Battalion began constructing a treadway bridge. The 1/401st GIR crossed the river near Le Grosseiller and were able to wade across due to the tides. The entire

The fields on either side of the causeway had been flooded in 1944 but were drained after the war, as seen here. Bridge No. 1 was over La Jourdan River, Bridge No. 2 over the Douve, Bridge No. 3 across La Groult stream, and Bridge No. 4 over La Madeleine. Saint-Côme-du-Mont can be seen in the upper left (6) and the Férme Pommenauque, also known as the Ingouf farm, in the lower left (5). (AHEC)

This Cointet obstacle, also known as a Belgian Gate, was used to obstruct the bridges along the Carentan causeway. This was the example at Bridge No. 1 nearest to Saint-Côme-du-Mont.

battalion was over the Douve by 0700hrs on June 10 and occupied the village of Brevands.

Gen. Taylor received information that unidentified troops, possibly American, had been spotted in the village of Auville-sur-le-Vey, about 3 miles southeast of Brevands. He ordered Col. Allen of the 1/401st GIR to send a company to investigate. Allen assigned the mission to Co. A and accompanied them to the village in the afternoon. After exchanging small-arms fire with German troops in the area, they reached the village around 1400hrs. There they found a small patrol from the 29th Infantry Division. This was the first link-up of Utah and Omaha Beaches. Allen and Maj. Paul Danahy, assistant division G-3, drove a jeep to the 29th Division command post and then on to V Corps headquarters. They briefed the V Corps commander, Maj. Gen. Leonard Gerow, of the situation with the 101st Airborne Division, and then returned to Auville. Co. A, 1/401st GIR returned to Brevands later in the day in preparation for the battalion's attack on Carentan.

Late on the night of June 10, the 2/327th GIR advanced down the road from Brevands to the northeastern outskirts of Carentan, with their left flank reaching the town of Saint-Hilaire-Petitville. They took up defensive positions along the Canal de Vire et Taute shortly before midnight.

On the morning of June 11, Co. G, 327th GIR began to advance down the Canal de Vire et Taute. The main issue in this sector was the complicated waterways where the canal ran parallel to the Douve River. As a result, much of the day was spent conducting improvised bridging operations to get the company southward. There was very little German resistance in this sector, in part because it was heavily flooded and in part because von der Heydte had decided to deploy his limited forces to other sectors, especially the west side of Carentan.

Bridge No. 4 over La Madeleine River, the final bridge on the Carentan causeway. Cole's troops were deployed around this bridge prior to the bayonet charge.

Crossing the causeway

On the night of June 9/10, Cole's 3/502nd PIR advanced to Le Pont de Douve

Lt. Col. Robert G. Cole, commander of 3/502nd PIR, was the only member of the 101st Airborne Division awarded the Medal of Honor for the Normandy fighting. He was killed in action during Operation *Market Garden* in September 1944.

at the start of the causeway. Lt. Gehauf led a reconnaissance party with ten other paratroopers, arriving at Bridge No. 2 around 0130hrs. Although there was engineer equipment evident, the bridge had not been rebuilt. Several engineers were under cover near the bridge and told Gehauf they had halted work when they came under fire from German artillery. The Gehauf patrol crossed the river in a small boat, at which point sporadic German artillery fire resumed. The patrol passed over Bridge No. 3 in the dark without incident and finally arrived at Bridge No. 4. This bridge had not been inspected before and Gehaulf was disturbed to find that it was firmly blocked by a Belgian Gate.

This type of obstacle, also known as a Cointet obstacle or Element C, had been developed for the Belgian Army and used for border defenses in 1940. The Germans had moved them to the Atlantikwall in 1943 and 1944, where they were used as obstacles. The Belgian Gate was fabricated from steel bars and was 10ft (3m) wide and 7ft (2m) high. They weighed 1.4 tonnes and were anchored at one end with a stake fixed into concrete, making them difficult to move without heavy equipment. Gehauf and his men were able to budge the obstacle away from one of the stone embankments on the bridge, creating a gap about 18in wide that a man could wriggle through. As they were trying to get through the obstacle, the Germans heard the commotion. A mortar shell fell nearby, followed by a flare and machine-gun fire. Gehauf sent a runner back to tell the lead company to silence the German machine guns with their mortars. The message was garbled and the runner told Col. Cole that Gehauf had said not to bring the battalion forward because the enemy fire was too heavy. The mistake made little difference, however, as with the growing dawn light, Lt. Col. Michaelis had decided to call off the predawn advance due to the engineer failure at Bridge No. 2.

A view of the Férme Pommenauque as seen from Bridge No. 4 at the end of the Carentan causeway. This is the view that Cole's men would have seen prior to the bayonet charge. (Paul Woodadge)

Battle of the causeway

Instead of waiting for nightfall, Cole's 3/502nd PIR were ordered to restart the advance over the causeway in the afternoon of June 10, on the presumption that German resistance in Carentan would be light. Artillery support was provided in the form of the 65th Armored FAB, the 377th Airborne FAB with one 75mm pack howitzer and two German howitzers, and the 907th Airborne FAB with 12 75mm pack howitzers. The main target was Pommenauque, the small hamlet on the southern edge of Bridge No. 4.

Col. Cole and Lt. Gehauf visited Bridge No. 2 around noon, finding that the engineers still had not bridged the gap. As a result, Cole instructed Capt. Robert Clements and some men from Co. G to create a foot bridge over the river using the engineer supplies nearby. A rickety foot bridge was improvised, and Gehauf was across with a patrol around 1500hrs. The Germans continued to lob artillery and mortar rounds at the site in a sporadic fashion, but fortunately for the American paratroopers, despite German artillery observers being able to see the bridge clearly from their observation post in the steeple of the church in Carentan, the 8./AR.191 was low on ammunition.

By late afternoon, Gehauf's patrol was on the far side of Bridge No. 4, the 1st Platoon of Co. G between Bridges Nos. 3 and 4, and the rest of the battalion strung out back to Pont de Douve. Over the course of three hours, the 3/502nd PIR, except for half of Co. H, crossed the flimsy foot bridge to the other side of the Douve. The Germans became aware of the American activity and began machine-gun and small-arms fire against the causeway. The heaviest fire came from Férme Pommenauque, also known as the Ingouf farm. The terrain past Bridge No. 4 was flat, so the farm buildings offered FJR.6 ample defensive opportunities. Besides the Fallschirmjäger in the farm buildings and surrounding area, other riflemen had taken up positions in the nearby marshes behind small hillocks and other terrain features. The German fire slowed the approach of the majority of Cole's battalion to Bridge No. 4.

Gehauf, realizing that the American artillery support was falling into empty fields behind Férme Pommenauque, asked Co. G to use their radio to readjust the fire. This was delayed and the fire did not begin to fall into the farm area until 2200hrs, as night was falling. The 3/502nd PIR had a modest amount of its own firepower and brought up two 60mm mortars and one 81mm mortar near Bridge No. 4. This was insufficient to significantly weaken the German defense, and the 3/502nd remained trapped on the causeway after dark.

Around 1800hrs, Col. Cole left his executive officer, Maj. John Stopka, in charge of the crossing operation at Bridge No. 2 and made his way to Co. G at Bridge No 4. There was no obvious way to advance down the causeway past Bridge No. 4 due to the constriction posed by the Belgian Gate and the intensity of German fire. He began talking to the commander of Co. G, Capt. Clements, about swimming his company across the marsh to the left, where the causeway would provide some cover to the German fire coming from the farm. However, this was eventually rejected when it was realized that there were German strongpoints on that side of the embankment.

In the meantime, Co. I was suffering a steady stream of casualties due to its exposure on the right side of the causeway, losing two platoon leaders and about 15 men. The situation improved after dark, when the Germans could no longer see the paratroopers on the causeway. Co. G continued to

THE BATTLE OF THE CARENTAN CAUSEWAY, JUNE 11, 1944

Cole's 3/502nd PIR secures the eastern bank of the Douve outside Carentan.

GERMAN

German defenses at start of the battle (11./FJR.6)

1. MG42 machine-gun position
2. 37mm antitank gun
3. 75mm Pak 40 antitank gun
4. 50mm light mortar

Fallschirmjäger-Regiment 6

5. 11.Kompanie, III./FJR.6 (morning positions)
6. KG Brunnklaus (6., 8./FJR.6)

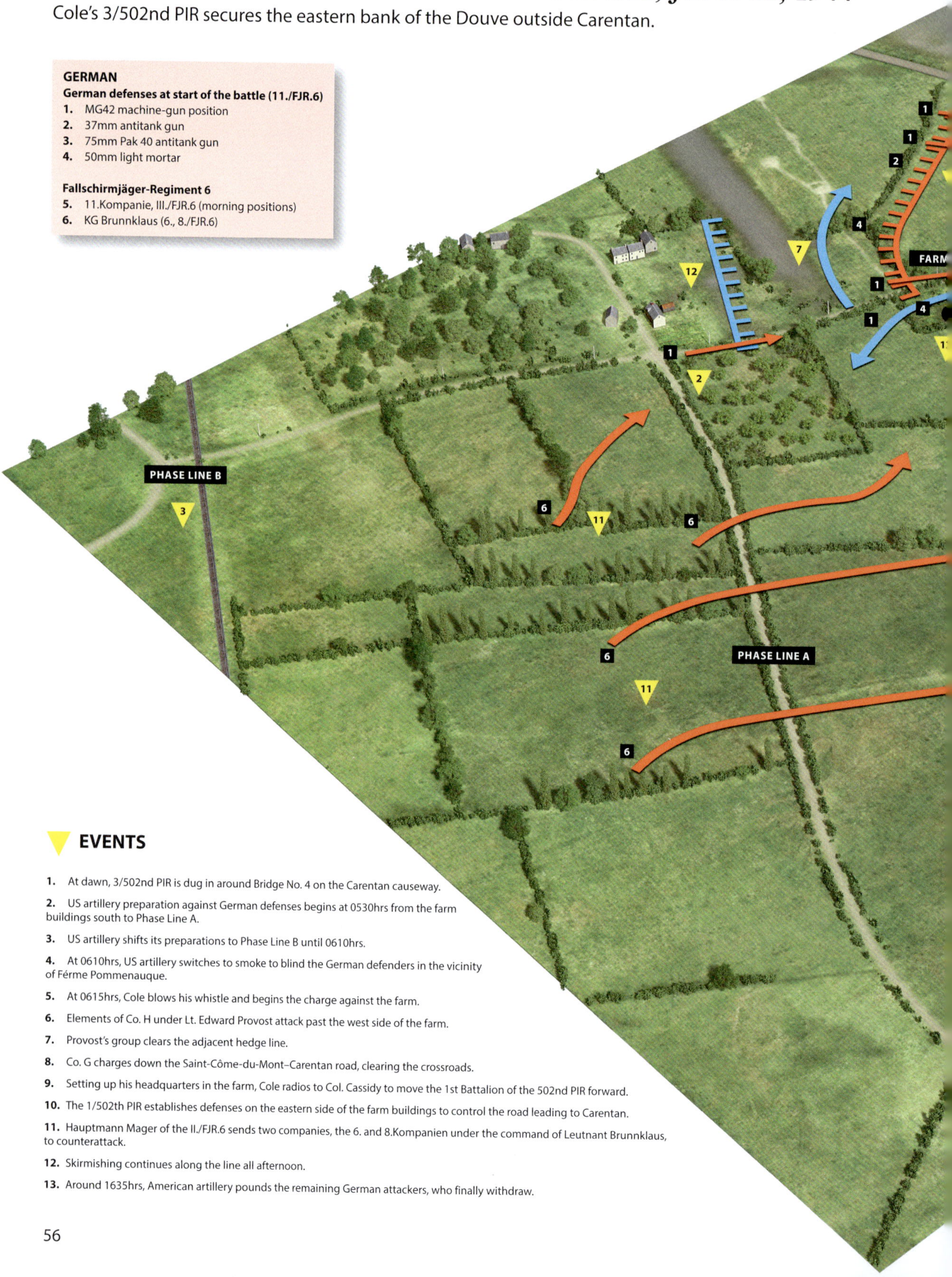

EVENTS

1. At dawn, 3/502nd PIR is dug in around Bridge No. 4 on the Carentan causeway.
2. US artillery preparation against German defenses begins at 0530hrs from the farm buildings south to Phase Line A.
3. US artillery shifts its preparations to Phase Line B until 0610hrs.
4. At 0610hrs, US artillery switches to smoke to blind the German defenders in the vicinity of Férme Pommenauque.
5. At 0615hrs, Cole blows his whistle and begins the charge against the farm.
6. Elements of Co. H under Lt. Edward Provost attack past the west side of the farm.
7. Provost's group clears the adjacent hedge line.
8. Co. G charges down the Saint-Côme-du-Mont–Carentan road, clearing the crossroads.
9. Setting up his headquarters in the farm, Cole radios to Col. Cassidy to move the 1st Battalion of the 502nd PIR forward.
10. The 1/502th PIR establishes defenses on the eastern side of the farm buildings to control the road leading to Carentan.
11. Hauptmann Mager of the II./FJR.6 sends two companies, the 6. and 8.Kompanien under the command of Leutnant Brunnklaus, to counterattack.
12. Skirmishing continues along the line all afternoon.
13. Around 1635hrs, American artillery pounds the remaining German attackers, who finally withdraw.

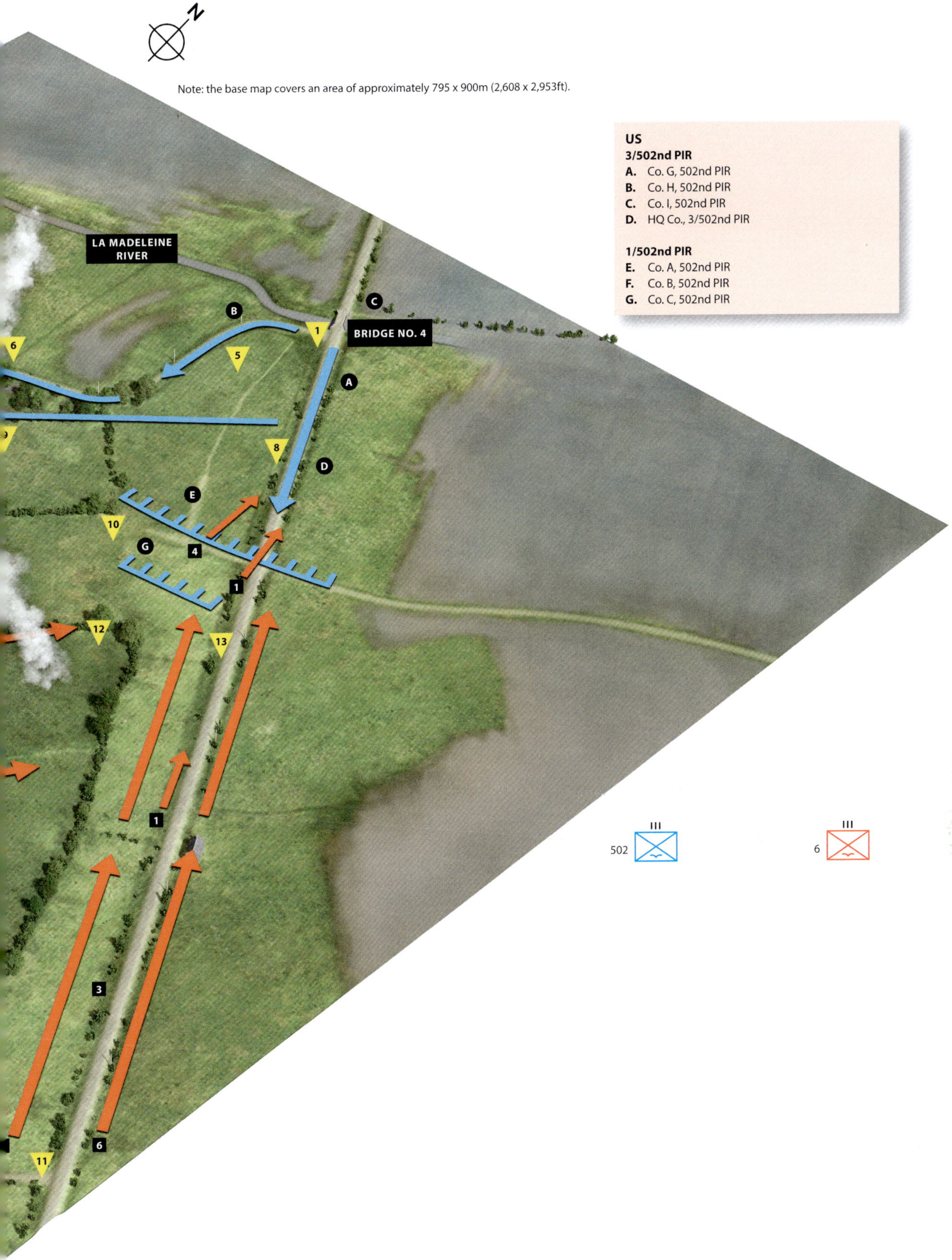
Note: the base map covers an area of approximately 795 x 900m (2,608 x 2,953ft).
N
US
3/502nd PIR
A. Co. G, 502nd PIR
B. Co. H, 502nd PIR
C. Co. I, 502nd PIR
D. HQ Co., 3/502nd PIR
1/502nd PIR
E. Co. A, 502nd PIR
F. Co. B, 502nd PIR
G. Co. C, 502nd PIR
LA MADELEINE RIVER
BRIDGE NO. 4
502
6

suffer from enemy fire as the Germans continued to pummel the area around Bridge No. 4.

Around 2330hrs, the paratroopers heard the approach of a German aircraft from the direction of Carentan. One aircraft, coming in at about 150ft, flew along the causeway and strafed the road, hitting the positions of Co. I. A second aircraft crossed perpendicular to the road and dropped six to eight small antipersonnel bombs. Co. I suffered about 30 casualties, of whom eight were dead or severely wounded. The identity of the attackers has remained a mystery. One soldier thought he saw its undercarriage, so this aircraft has been identified as a Ju-87 Stuka. However, there were no Stukas in Normandy at the time. The most likely candidates for the attack were the Fw-190A fighter-bombers of III./Schlachtgeschwader 4, a specialized night attack formation, which also happened to be based at the closest Luftwaffe airfield. According to unit records, it staged about 40 sorties along the Normandy beachhead that night, of which the Carentan attack may have been one.

After this rare German air attack, the fighting quietened down. The night was clear and the moon eventually rose, giving the paratroopers a clear view of Carentan a few minutes further down the road. In the early morning hours, Cole continued to prod the platoon commanders to get their men past the Belgian Gate and down the causeway beyond. Co. H substituted for Co. G in taking the lead; Co. I was still reeling from the casualties suffered while crossing the causeway and the subsequent air attack. Cole consulted with Sink during the night, and they agreed to continue the attack, since the battalion would be badly exposed if it tried to withdraw back over the causeway after daylight on June 11. At the time, Cole had about 265 paratroopers in Co. G, Co. H, and the HQ Co., and was facing about two companies of Fallschirmjäger in camouflaged strongpoints. This ratio of forces did not favor the attacker.

A pencil sketch by a member of the 101st Airborne Division showing the exposed nature of the Carentan causeway, with little cover except for a few stunted poplar trees.

As dawn broke, Cole was forward with Co. H along with the artillery liaison officer, Capt. Rosemond. Cole told Rosemond to radio the supporting artillery and have them engage the farm house and neighboring hedges. Rosemond told Cole that he could not get the fire mission approved as the artillery commander was not present. Exasperated, Cole said, "Goddamn it! We need artillery fire and we can't wait for a general!" Rosemond was more forceful in his next request, and the first salvo struck near the farm house about 15 minutes later.

The artillery preparation began around 0530hrs and lasted until shortly before 0600hrs. In spite of the artillery preparation, there was intense German small-arms fire whenever there was any movement on the American side. Rosemond asked the artillery to switch from air-burst to time-delay fuses, hoping that this would improve the effect of the artillery. However, it seemed to make little difference.

By this stage, Cole's executive officer, Maj. Stopka, had reached the head of the column on the road opposite Cole. Cole yelled across the road that he intended to call down smoke on the German positions and then stage a bayonet charge against the farm. Stopka replied "OK" and word was passed to the scattered platoons to fix bayonets. It took another 15–20 minutes for the smoke barrage to arrive. In the meantime, the American mortar teams attempted to pick out the most dangerous German machine-gun strongpoints and knock them out before the charge. A number of paratroopers managed to infiltrate forward and attack the isolated German positions with hand-grenades. Cole told Stopka to be ready at 0615hrs and the artillery was instructed to shift their fire from the farm buildings back to the railroad line behind the farm.

At 0615hrs, Cole blew his whistle and charged forward out of the ditch, armed with a .45 cal pistol. Only about 20 men followed him, including his radio-operator, T/5 Robert Doran. Across the road, Stopka and another 50 men ran forward, with Stopka shouting, "Let's go! Over the hedge." Co. G was well represented in the bayonet charge, but there were few paratroopers from Co. H or HQ Company. After a few hundred feet, Cole stopped and looked back. He was shocked to see how few men had followed. Many were advancing single file, making them more vulnerable to German fire. Cole shouted and told them to fan out, but they misunderstood and hit the dirt. Cole fired his .45 cal pistol wildly toward the farm to encourage others to follow. Stopka ran back and tried to get more men moving. Many paratroopers had never heard the whistle amid the din of the shelling, while other platoons had never received the instructions regarding the planned bayonet charge.

Gradually, more and more paratroopers from Co. H and the HQ Company joined the charge. As the momentum gradually built up, the paratroopers could see the farm emerging from the smoke. Cole leapt over a hedge near the farm building, only to end up shoulder-deep in an irrigation ditch. He warned Doran to avoid it, as the radio would be damaged by the water, and Doran avoided the ditch with a single leap. By this point, other paratroopers were running past Cole. The first two soldiers into the farm house, 1st Sgt. Kenneth Sprecker and Pvt. Roach of Co. H, shot the lock off the door and ran inside. They found the house empty except for a few dead Germans. Exiting the building, they caught two Fallschirmjäger outside and Sprecker hit both of them with his .45 cal Thompson submachine gun.

GRAHAM TURNER

THE PARATROOPER CHARGE AT THE CARENTAN CAUSEWAY, JUNE 11, 1944 (PP.60–61)

On the morning of June 11, Lt. Col. Robert Cole **(1)** had his depleted 3rd Battalion, 502nd PIR, deployed near Bridge No. 4 at the southern end of the Carentan causeway near the Pommenauque suburb of Carentan. His troops were under continual small-arms and mortar fire by entrenched troops of the FJR.6, centered around the Férme Pommenauque, also known as the Ingouf farm. To overcome the German defenses, Cole requested that supporting artillery douse the farm complex with smoke rounds. He instructed his troops to fix bayonets and prepare to charge the farm once the smoke had sufficiently obscured the approaches. At 0615hrs, Cole blew his whistle and charged forward out of the ditch, armed with a .45 cal pistol **(2)**. He was followed by his radioman, T/5 Robert Doran, equipped with an SCR-300 walkie-talkie FM radio **(3)**. Due to confusion over the plans, at first only about 20 men followed Cole. He continued to run toward the farm, firing his .45 cal pistol. Eventually, more troops followed, prodded on by his example as well as by his executive officer, Maj. John Stopka. The charge eventually included about 100 paratroopers, who managed to overwhelm the positions of the 11./FJR.6 holding the farm.

The paratroopers are armed primarily with the M1 Garand rifle **(4)**, the same weapon used by regular US Army infantry units. Some paratroopers were issued the M1A1 carbine. This was a specialized version of the carbine with a folding stock to make it easier to be stowed for airborne drops. The paratroopers had a different uniform than regular US infantry or the glider infantry of the 101st Airborne Division. It was distinguished by additional pockets to carry the paratrooper's gear **(5)**. Prior to the Normandy air landings, the battledress was impregnated with a type of wax coating intended to seal it against the possible German use of chemical weapons. The paratroopers were also issued with a different version of the standard M1 helmet that had reinforced straps and a leather chin cup to ensure it remained in place during the parachute drop. The battalions of the 101st Airborne Division adopted special insignia painted on the side of their helmets, in this case a heart **(6)**. Paratroopers were also authorized to wear Corcoran leather jump boots that offered better ankle protection during landing **(7)**.

One of the remaining strongpoints was a hedge near the house where the Fallschirmjäger had dug in a machine gun. They were still firing on the paratroopers when a squad from Co. H, led by Lt. Edward Provost, snuck up on them and hurled grenades into the position. Nearby was an old 37mm antitank gun strongpoint that was cleared by Provost's men. Upon reaching a hedge that bordered the orchard behind the house, Provost and his men spotted about 20 Fallschirmjäger milling around. The paratroopers immediately fired on them, but Provost was wounded in the ensuing skirmish. Sgt. Sprecker appeared and led the clearing of the orchard.

Some of the surviving Fallschirmjäger used the cover of the smoke to withdraw from the farm through the orchard toward the railway line into Carentan. Eventually, most of the paratroopers from all four companies converged on the farm house and adjoining buildings. Cole directed Co. G and Co. I to set up defenses in a nearby brush pile. Co. H and the HQ Company were ordered to the right side of the house. By this stage, Cole's 3/502nd PIR had suffered so many casualties that he doubted he could hold the farm position, and certainly not complete the mission of seizing Hill 30. He sent a runner back, instructing Col. Patrick Cassidy to move the 1st Battalion forward.

While Cole's charge had been taking shape, the situation on the causeway had been largely cleared. Engineers had finally established a bridge over Bridge No. 2 and had pushed aside the Belgian Gate on Bridge No. 4. This permitted the dispatch of a truck to help bring back the wounded from Cole's command.

Col. Cassidy began moving the 1/502nd PIR over the causeway as the first wave of wounded paratroopers started filtering back. Cassidy believed that Cole's battalion had broken the German resistance, at the cost of his own unit. His plan was to move the 1/502nd PIR through the farm buildings and

Following the battle for the Férme Pommenauque, men of the 2/502nd PIR display a captured flag. From left to right are Lt. Col. Robert Cole, 1st Sgt. Hubert Odom, SSgt. Robert O'Reilly, and Maj. John P. Stopka.

advance directly on Hill 30, the principal objective. Cassidy soon realized he had underestimated the strength of the remaining German forces. His vanguard, Co. B, took heavy German machine-gun fire from remaining positions near the railway line to the south. They were followed by Co. A, which took even heavier casualties when it was caught by a mortar and artillery barrage in the open field between Bridge No. 4 and the farm around 1100hrs. To compound the problem, Capt. Rosemond, the forward artillery observer, was having a difficult time calling in artillery support as the area around the farm consisted of small fields edged in bocage, with no clear evidence whether they were held by American or German forces.

With the arrival of Co. C, Cassidy eventually created a set of defenses around the farmyard held by Cole's 3/502nd PIR. Co. B was assigned to the fields south of the farmyard while Cos. A and C formed a double defense line on either side of a cabbage patch along the N13 Saint-Côme-du-Mont–Carentan road.

While the American paratroopers were reinforcing their toe-hold around the Férme Pommenauque, the Germans were planning to retake the farm. Hauptmann Mager of the II./FJR.6 sent two companies, the 6. and 8.Kompanien under the command of Leutnant Brunnklaus, to redeem the situation. Von der Heydte ordered other units to the scene, but it was largely left to the overextended Fallschirmjäger to attempt to recapture the farm.

Around noon, Lt. Col. Michaelis radioed Cole and Cassidy that the Germans had requested a truce. The details of who requested the truce from the German side remains a mystery. Maj. Douglas Davidson, the regimental surgeon, served as the US envoy and attempted to walk into Carentan to speak with von der Heydte. However, he was stopped by Hauptmann Mager, who responded to his request for a surrender with a negative response, saying, "Would you surrender?" Davidson returned to the American positions around 1300hrs. Moments later, the German lines erupted in heavy fire, particularly from the mortars and artillery located on Hill 30. The German fire eventually subsided and Rosemond concluded that the German artillery batteries had been reduced to only two howitzers. However, mortar fire remained steady through the afternoon. German machine-gun positions on either flank still managed to prevent the US side from sending jeeps down the causeway. Instead, ammunition boxes were passed along the road by wounded paratroopers in trenches along the elevated highway.

By late afternoon, American artillery support had halted after the Germans began jamming the radio that Rosemond had been using to communicate with the 502nd PIR headquarters. Another problem was that the US artillery battalions had run low on ammunition. Around 1630hrs, Rosemond was finally able to get through to the regimental headquarters and warned them that unless they got more support, they would have to retreat back over the causeway. By this stage, the divisional artillery had received more ammunition and began a hasty bombardment of the area around the farm. The barrage lasted only five minutes, and some of it fell short, impacting within the American lines. Nevertheless, it finally shattered the German resolve.

Once the small-arms fire had died down, Cole sent out two patrols to determine the situation. There was still some machine-gun fire from a distance, but the Fallschirmjäger had withdrawn, leaving behind their dead. At 2000hrs, the 2/502nd PIR arrived and took over from Cole's 3/502nd

PIR. Less than 130 men of Cole's command from the original 250 marched back over the causeway to Saint-Côme-du-Mont around dusk.

The German withdrawal

What was not apparent to Cole and Cassidy was that the situation on the German side was even more desperate. The 11.Kompanie of FJR.6, which had been the main body of the original German defenses, suffered 114 casualties that day. The shortage of machine-gun ammunition became so severe that all rifle ammunition was collected for the machine-gun teams, leaving the Fallschirmjäger armed only with pistols or weapons using pistol ammunition, such as the MP40 submachine gun. Von der Heydte again pleaded with the 84.AK for an ammunition delivery. As if that was not enough, he received reports that Ost-Bataillon.635 had withdrawn from its positions and that American tanks had been spotted on the N13 highway east of Carentan around Saint-Hilaire-Petitville. There were indeed Americans at Saint-Hilaire, but no tanks, the town being weakly held by the 327th GIR after their previous actions on June 10. Von der Heydte consulted with his two battalion commanders. Trebes said that he doubted they could hold another day, while Mager was more equivocal. Von der Heydte later wrote that it was the American capture of the Férme Pommenauque and the resultant decimation of his two remaining Fallschirmjäger battalions that convinced him that the defense of Carentan was on the verge of collapse. The two Fallschirmjäger battalions had lost most of their officers and NCOs.

In light of these circumstances, von der Heydte believed that his regiment would be overwhelmed and forced to surrender to the Americans if they tried holding Carentan another day. He had been told the day before to expect the arrival of 17.SS-Pz.Gren.Div. for a counterattack around 1500hrs that afternoon, but there were no signs of this unit. In mid-afternoon, he informed his two battalion commanders as well as other detachment

The Germans withdrew from Carentan on the evening of June 11, taking up new defensive positions on Hill 30 on the southern outskirts of town. Hill 30 is in the center of this aerial photo, bisected by the Carentan–Périers road, today's D971.

CAPTURE OF CARENTAN, JUNE 12, 1944

Von der Heydte's plan to control Hill 30 fails.

GERMAN

1. Fallschirmjäger-Regiment.6
2. Artillerie-Gruppe Rock
3. Ost.Bataillon.439
4. Ost.Bataillon.635
5. III./GR.1058 (91.LL-Div.)
6. II./GR.914 (352.Inf.Div.)

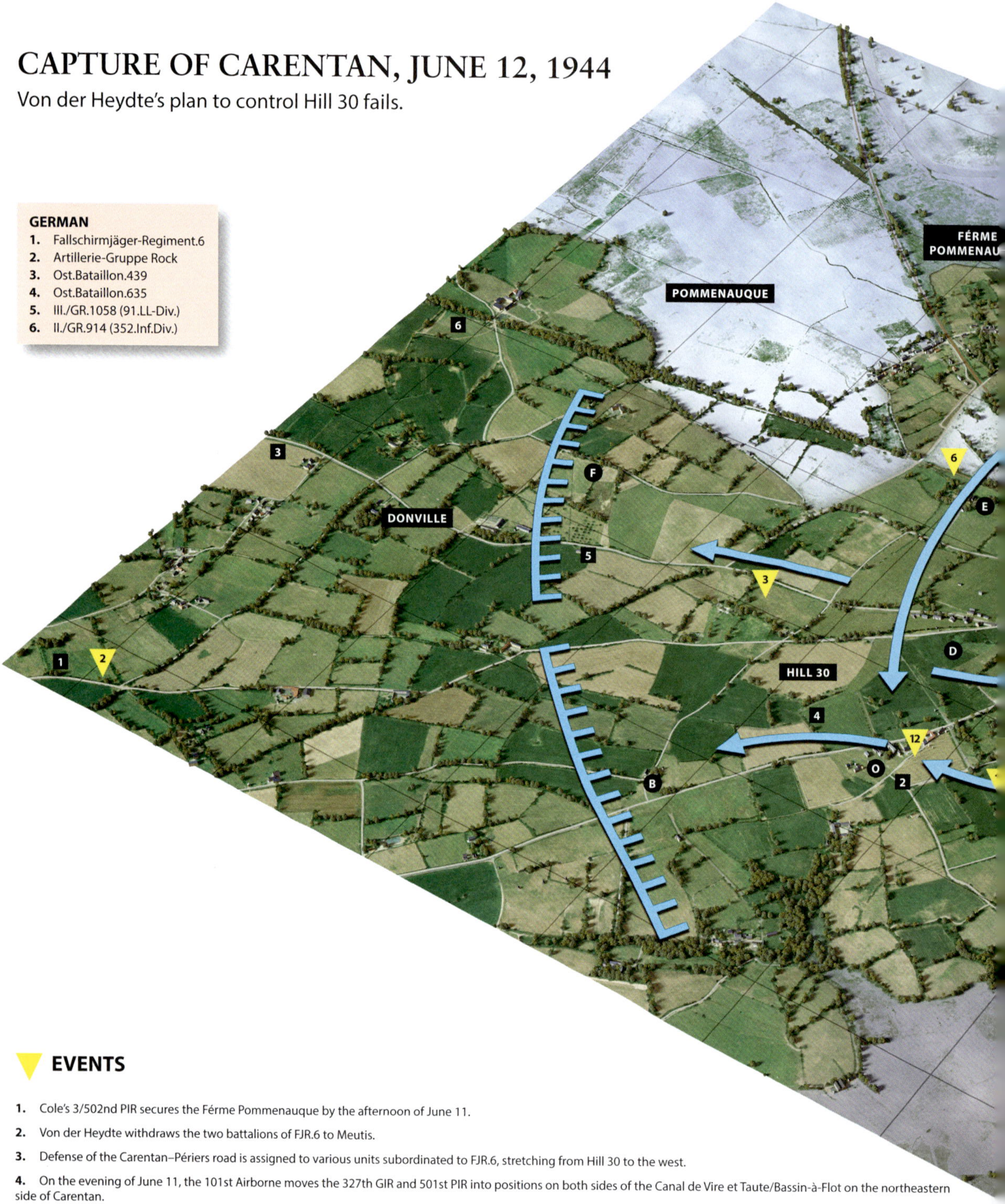

EVENTS

1. Cole's 3/502nd PIR secures the Férme Pommenauque by the afternoon of June 11.
2. Von der Heydte withdraws the two battalions of FJR.6 to Meutis.
3. Defense of the Carentan–Périers road is assigned to various units subordinated to FJR.6, stretching from Hill 30 to the west.
4. On the evening of June 11, the 101st Airborne moves the 327th GIR and 501st PIR into positions on both sides of the Canal de Vire et Taute/Bassin-à-Flot on the northeastern side of Carentan.
5. The 506th PIR moves across the causeway during the evening of June 11 in preparation for the next day's attack.
6. The 506th PIR moves toward Hill 30 on the night of June 11/12.
7. The 1/401st GIR starts advancing southward along the Bassin-à-Flot waterway at 0500hrs.
8. Cos. E and F, 506th PIR, advance into Carentan starting at 0500hrs, encountering German stragglers.
9. Carentan is largely cleared by 1000hrs with very light casualties. The main problem area is the railroad station at the southern side of the town.
10. The 501st PIR moves against Hill 30 across flooded fields, receiving concentrated mortar, machine-gun, and 20mm Flak fire from Artillerie-Gruppe Rock on Hill 30.
11. 3/501st PIR overruns German defenses on Hill 30 and Ost.Bataillon.439 flees.
12. Von der Heydte orders Hauptmann Hauch to recapture the hill using the 15.Pionier-Kompanie/FJR.6, but the attack is overwhelmed by an American artillery barrage.

Note: gridlines are shown at intervals of 500m (1,640ft).

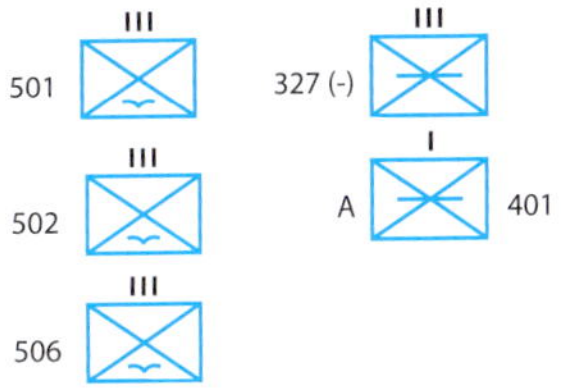

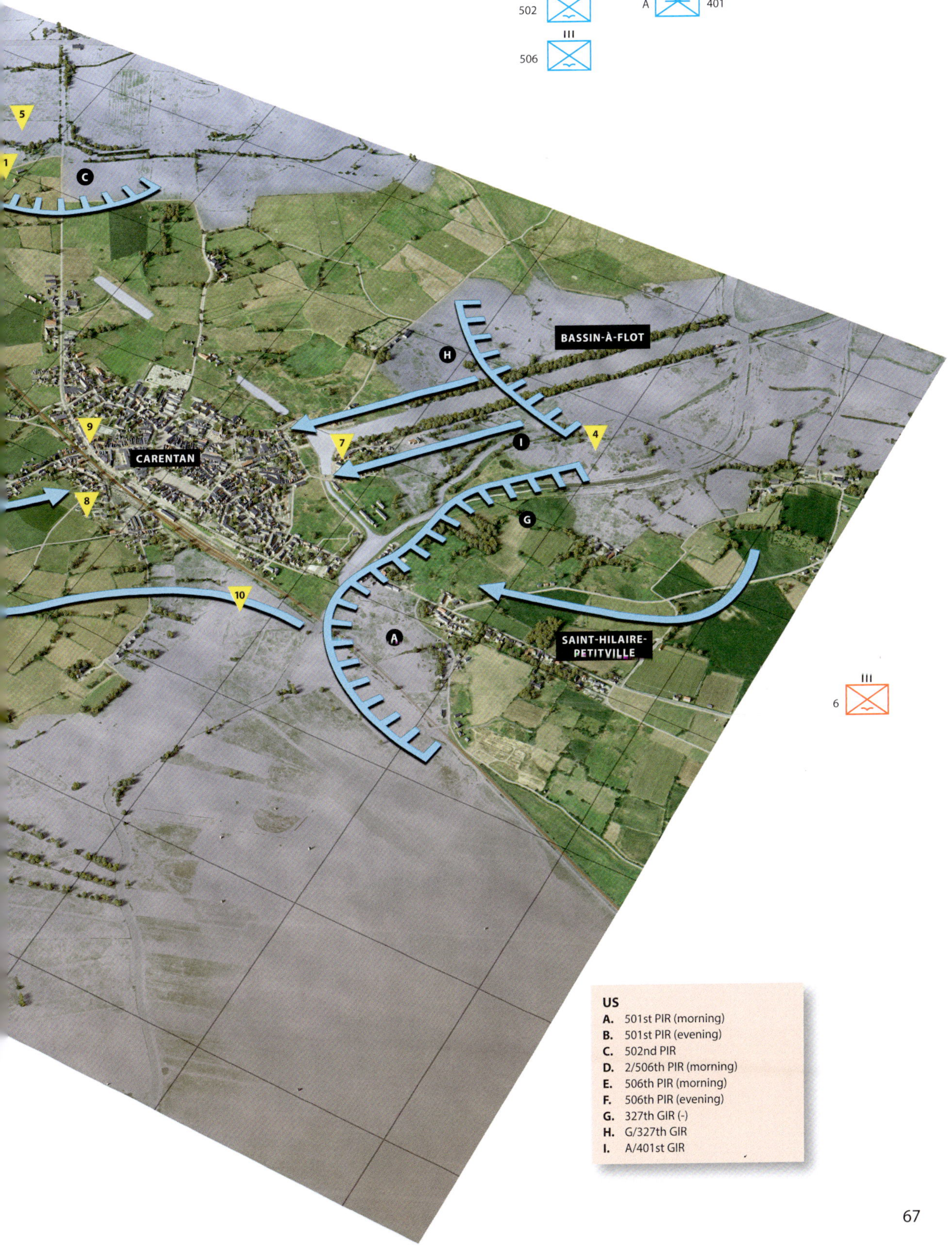

A jeep of the 81st Airborne AA Battalion tows a 6-pdr (57mm) airborne antitank gun on Rue Holgate, near the intersection with Route N13/Rue de Saint-Côme, on June 12, to reinforce the defenses facing Périers, where German forces were massing. Three batteries of this battalion used the British lightweight airborne version of the 6-pdr antitank gun instead of the heavier US M1 57mm antitank gun.

commanders that Fallschirmjäger-Regiment.6 would begin withdrawing to Hill 30 south of the town at 1600hrs. His adjutant, Hauptmann Pelser, was given the thankless task of contacting 84.AK headquarters and informing them.

In a postwar report written for the US Army, von der Heydte wrote that he had informed the 84.AK of his decision to withdraw from Carentan, and that the corps had "approved this step." Furthermore, he claimed that he had not been informed by 84.AK that the 17.SS-Panzergrenadier-Division was on the verge of arriving in Carentan to secure the town. In response, Generalleutnant Max Pemsel, the chief-of-staff of AOK.7 in 1944, penned a rebuttal. He insisted that von der Heydte had been informed personally of the arrival of the 17.SS-Pz.Gren.Div. on June 10 by the chief-of-staff of the 84.AK, Oberstleutnant Friedrich von Criegern. Pemsel also described the withdrawal from Carentan as "premature" and not authorized by either 84.AK or AOK.7. But he rationalized von der Heydte's actions: "As a result of the preceding severe and disastrous fighting, the commander of FJR.6 suffered a temporary physical and mental breakdown. The fact that his command of the regiment had so far been outstanding and that he made a speedy recovery prevented the FJR.6 commander from being punished or relieved of his command."

Mager and Trebes were instructed to undertake the retreat as quietly as possible and to leave behind a few rearguards to ensure that the Americans did not take advantage of the withdrawal. It was these rearguards who conducted the last volley of fire against Cole's and Cassidy's men in the afternoon.

The commander of 17.SS-Pz.Gen.Div., SS-Brigadeführer Ostendorff, met von der Heydte in Carentan during the afternoon after the retreat order had been issued. Von der Heydte asked Ostendorff to send a relief column to Carentan as soon as possible due to the desperate circumstances of FJR.6. Ostendorff refused, noting that his unit was still strung out on the roads south of Carentan and that none could arrive before nightfall. The idea of staging an attack with inexperienced units at night, with no familiarity of the terrain and with no artillery support, was a recipe for disaster. Ostendorff instead suggested that he would try to bring up forces as quickly as possible during the daylight hours of June 12. Both Ostendorff and von der Heydte conducted a brief reconnaissance to determine the best terrain for the counterattack.

Paratroopers of the 101st Airborne Division on a Luftwaffe Volkswagen Kubelwagen, captured from FJR.6, drive through Carentan on June 12 at the intersection of Rue Holgate and Route N13/Rue de Saint-Côme.

On the night of June 11/12, the Luftwaffe conducted an airdrop of about 13 tonnes of

A column from the 101st Airborne Division on Rue Holgate in Carentan on June 12. The jeep is from the 326th Airborne Medical Company and is followed by a captured German truck also in use by the medics.

ammunition and supplies to FJR.6 in a field outside the town of Raids to the southwest of Carentan. It was a day too late.

The capture of Carentan

Von der Heydte assigned the defense of Hill 30 to Ost-Bataillon.439, Ost-Bataillon.635, and the assortment of other units that had accumulated under his command over the preceding days. Both II./ and III./FJR.6 were sent deeper to the rear to rehabilitate after the bruising battle on June 11. Von der Heydte did not think that the Americans would attack until June 13, by which time he planned to move his two battalions of FJR.6 back into the front lines. In his postwar report, he acknowledged that this was a mistake as the Soviet PoWs of the Ost-Bataillone did not have the resolve to resist the paratrooper attack.

By the late evening of June 11, the 101st Airborne had moved the 327th/401st GIR and the 501st PIR into positions on both sides of the Canal de Vire et Taute on the northeastern corner of Carentan. Gen. McAullife led the operation to capture Carentan. The original plan was to use the 502nd PIR to form the southern pincer of the attack on the town. However, Lt. Col. Michaelis asked the divisional headquarters to use another regiment due to the extent of the casualties in the 502nd PIR after the past two days of fighting along "Purple Heart

Troops of the 1/401st GIR march through Carentan near the Place de la Republique on June 14 following the capture of the town. The 327th GIR entered the town through its northern and northeastern streets.

The 506th PIR developed a reputation as the "airborne cavalry" for its extensive use of captured German vehicles. This is a British Morris-Commercial 15cwt General Service lorry, captured by the Wehrmacht in the 1940 campaign and used as an ambulance. It is followed by a captured motorcycle with sidecar and trailer in the Carentan area on June 17.

Lane" – the Carentan causeway. The 506th PIR was selected to carry out the southern attack against Hill 30.

The 506th PIR began moving across the causeway during the evening of June 11, passing through the 502nd PIR positions in Pommenauque, and finally stopping about a mile south of Hill 30. One account of the 101st Airborne Division jokingly referred to the 506th PIR at this point as "airborne cavalry," as it had collected so many German vehicles and horses. This movement put the 506th PIR in control of the main roads leading out of Carentan to the south, while the 327th GIR and 501st PIR already controlled most of the highways north and east. Col. Sink set up his command post near the two forward battalions of the 506th PIR.

The 101st Airborne Division sent patrols toward Carentan at first light on June 12. The patrols encountered scattered rifle fire, but it appeared that the main German force had withdrawn and left behind a small rearguard. The 1/401st GIR started advancing southward along the Bassin-à-Flot waterway at 0500hrs. Col. Harper and Gen. Taylor accompanied them, and the battalion was first into town by 0700hrs after dealing with scattered snipers.

The 2/506th PIR also started advancing at 0500hrs while the 1/506th PIR cleared the area around Sink's regimental command post. Co. F led the 506th PIR into the town amid desultory mortar and sniper fire. It was followed by Co. E, which suffered nine casualties from mortar and small-arms fire during their advance. Lt. Dick Winters of Co. E shifted his company to the right to deal with German stragglers. Meanwhile, Co. F advanced swiftly into town and contacted the 327th GIR by radio to avoid a collision of the two forces. There was a lot of small-arms fire by the airborne troops against potential sniper positions, but the town was empty of German forces by mid-morning. Carentan was cleared by 1000hrs, at a cost of very light casualties. The main problem area was the railroad station at the southern side of the town.

The first serious encounters with German defenses occurred south of the town as the 501st PIR moved against Hill 30. The regiment crossed the

On June 13, Brigadeführer Werner Ostendorff (left), the 17.SS-Pz.Gren.Div. commander, discusses plans for the Carentan attack with Major Friedrich von der Heydte (center), commander of FJR.6. The officer on the right is SS-Sturmbannführer Eugen Holzapfel, a liaison officer from SS-Aufklärungs-Abt.17.

Canal de Vire et Taute after a preliminary artillery barrage accompanied by smoke rounds. The regiment had not anticipated the extent of the flooding beyond the canal, finding much of the area completely inundated. As Co. H, 501st PIR emerged from the smoke, they were hit by concentrated mortar, machine gun, and 20mm Flak fire from Artillerie-Gruppe Rock on Hill 30. The 3/501st PIR commander, Lt. Col. Ewell, later remarked that, "The strain of wading across a shallow pond with 20mm spraying the water was terrific. We were really shot. I was so damn exhausted emotionally that I just didn't care about anything. The people who did the real fighting were worse. The fighting, as far as I personally was concerned, was the most trying that I went through in all our fighting in

A Fallschirmjäger of FJR.6 is seen advancing, with a StuG IV assault gun of SS-Panzer.Abt.17 behind him, during the July 13 attack toward Carentan.

German attack toward Carentan, morning of June 13

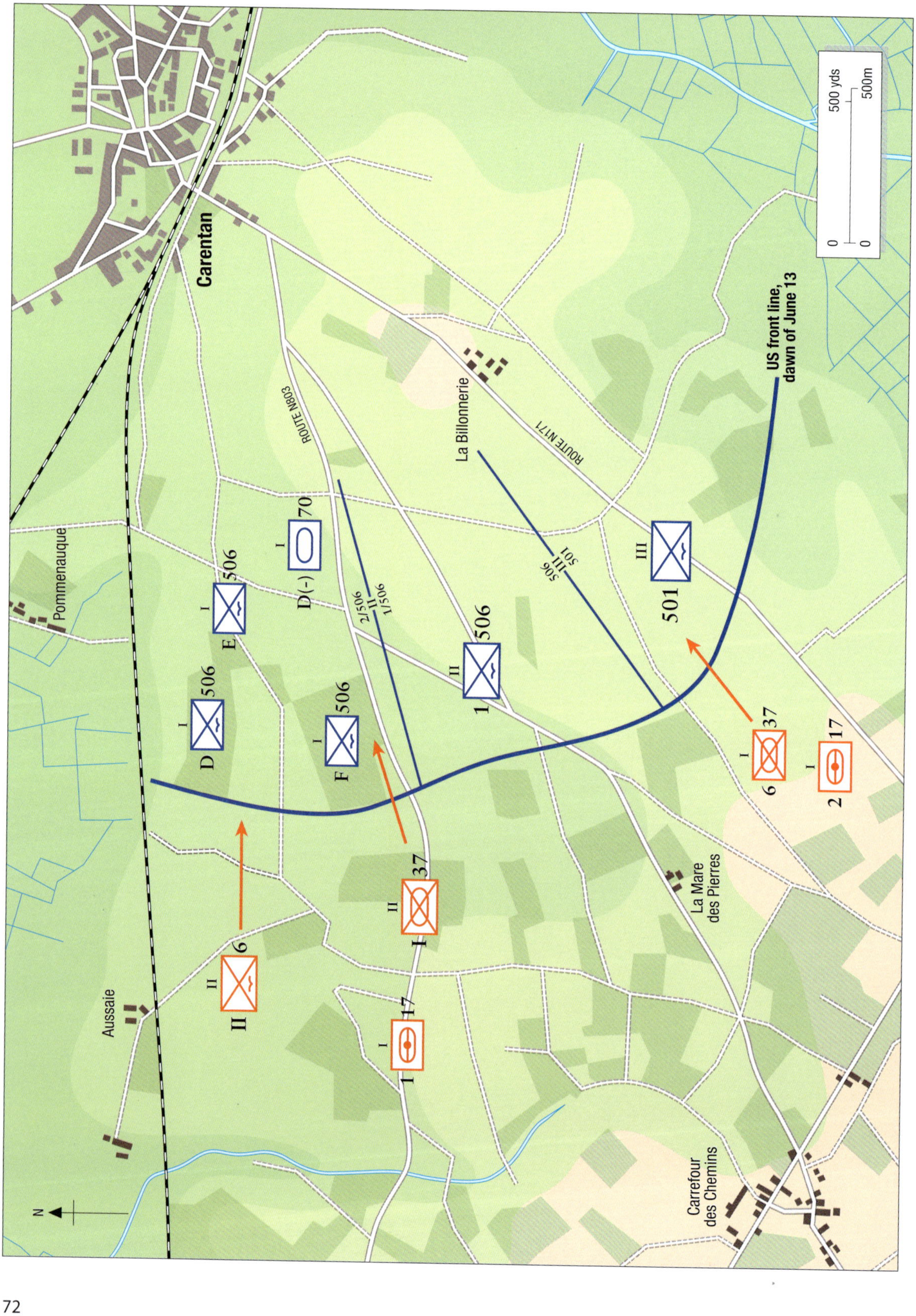

A section from 10./FJR.6 under Gefreiter Georg Schober in the bocage, probably during the June 13 fighting.

Europe." Some paratroopers of Co. H had already reached the base of Hill 30 and charged forward, overrunning the 20mm Flak guns.

In the meantime, Co. I, 501st PIR advanced along the southern outskirts of Carentan past the railroad station, then turned southward to the base of Hill 30. It was initially halted by small-arms fire from the hill, but supporting artillery began pummeling the German positions. What the paratroopers did not know was that the Ost-Bataillon holding the hill had mostly fled at the sight of the paratrooper advance. Von der Heydte ordered Hauptmann Hauch to recapture the hill using the 15.Pionier-Kompanie, but the attack was enveloped by the American artillery barrage and hardly noticed by the 501st PIR. Hill 30, intended to be the lynchpin of the new German defense line, had fallen into American hands.

Troops of 1./SS-Pz.Gren.Rgt.37 advancing toward Carentan on June 13.

GRAHAM TURNER

GERMAN ATTACK ON CARENTAN, JUNE 13, 1944 (PP.74–75)

The German attack on Carentan on June 13 was spearheaded by a company of StuG IV assault guns **(1)** of the SS-Panzer-Abt.17. In spite of the unit designation, the Panzer regiments in Panzergrenadier divisions in 1944 usually had StuG III or StuG IV assault guns instead of tanks. The StuG III was by far the most common type of assault gun and was based on the PzKpfw III tank. The StuG IV as seen here had a similar superstructure and gun, but was fitted to the PzKpfw IV chassis. It can be most easily distinguished by the driver's compartment at the forward left side of the superstructure that extends farther forward than on the StuG III **(2)**. These assault guns could be fitted with side-skirt armor, but most photos from the Normandy fighting indicate that this was not carried **(3)**. It was developed mainly to shield the side armor of the assault guns from Soviet antitank rifles, and so had little utility in Normandy where such weapons were not present. Some German tanks did use the armor plates, which they mistakenly called "bazooka skirts" – protection from bazookas was not their actual intention.

The 1.Kompanie of SS-Panzer-Abt.17 attacked toward the northwestern corner of Carentan, hitting Cos. E and F of the 506th PIR. The 2.Kompanie attacked along Route N171 toward the southeastern corner of Carentan. The German assault guns were accompanied by Panzergrenadiers of the 17.SS-Pz.Gren. Div. **(4)**. The main force was from I./SS-Pz.Gren.Regt.37, but the 6.Kompanie of II./SS-Pz.Gren.Regt.37 took part on the right flank of the attack. This was the combat debut of this division, and the troops were unaccustomed to fighting in the Normandy hedgerow country. The situation was not helped by the weather that day, which was very rainy and overcast, obscuring the battlefield.

THE CARENTAN COUNTERATTACK

In the days after the Allied invasion, Rommel planned to stage a major Panzer counteroffensive to push the Allies back into the sea. Panzer divisions were moved to Normandy and consolidated under Panzergruppe West. Rommel's focus wavered over the next few days. On June 9, he decided that his forces in the Caen sector would shift to the defensive in order to mobilize forces to defeat the US Army's drive on the port of Cherbourg. British intelligence discovered the location of the Panzergruppe West command post and attacked it with fighter-bombers on June 10. This derailed any short-term plans for a great Panzer counterattack. On June 11, Rommel again emphasized the need to swap infantry divisions for Panzer divisions in the Caen sector facing the British to shift the focus to the Cherbourg–Montebourg–Carentan sector. The fall of Carentan on June 11 infuriated Hitler, who the following day issued one of his special directives that such strongpoints must never again be surrendered and that the garrison must fight to the death. Facing Hitler's wrath, Rommel ordered 84.AK to immediately recapture Carentan.

The 84.AK could barely manage to hold the line against the US Army's VII Corps, so Rommel shifted more resources to the Cotentin peninsula. Meindl's II.Fallschirmjäger-Korps was subordinated to 84.AK on June 12, even though few of its authorized divisions had yet arrived within striking distance of Carentan. Its only mobile formation was the 17.SS-Pz.Gren.Div. "Götz von Berlichingen." On D-Day, this division was stationed at Thouars, south of the Loire River in western France and 380km from Carentan. The division had a severe shortage of trucks, with only 50 on hand on June 1 compared to an authorized strength of 874. As a result, its transfer to Normandy was conducted by various means, with two of its six infantry battalions using bicycles, the others employing divisional vehicles and trucks taken from the French, and the heavy elements being transported by railway. The railway journey was abruptly ended by Allied air attacks barely 100km into the journey, with the trains being bombed at La Flèche and Montreuil-Bellay and forced to prematurely disembark due to blown bridges and other interruptions.

The 84.AK intended to start the attack on Carentan at 1500hrs on July 12. Since insufficient forces had arrived by that time, however, it was postponed a day until June 13. The Luftwaffe was instructed to conduct bombing attacks against targets around the town in the predawn hours of June 13; these never occurred. Due to the slow pace of arrival, the counterattack was skimpy, based around I./SS-Pz.Gren.Regt.37, reinforced with 6./Pz.Gren. Regt.37, two companies of assault guns of SS-Panzer-Abt.17, and a section from the Sf-Kompanie/SS-Panzerjäger-Abt.17 with Marder tank destroyers. Fire support came from I./SS-Artillerie-Regiment.17. These forces were supported by Kampfgruppe Heintz, from the 275.Infanterie-Division. KG Heintz was given no role in the attack, but rather was assigned to defend the sector southeast of Carentan to protect the rear of the attack force. Von der Heydte's FJR.6 was split into its two surviving battalions, with II./FJR.6 assigned to I./SS-Pz.Gren.Rgt.37 and the III./FJR.6 placed in divisional reserve.

The first elements of the regiment, Obersturmführer Tetzmann's 6.Kompanie from II./SS-Pz.Gren.Rgt.37, arrived in the area on the morning of June 12 after a long bicycle trip. It then began marching toward

Around 1400hrs on June 13, three StuG IV assault guns of 2./SS-Panzer.Abt.17 were retreating past the hamlet of La Gallioterie on the N171 Carentan–Périers road at the intersection of today's route D903 and D971, south of Carentan, when they were ambushed by the 101st Airborne Division. One of the 6-pdr antitank guns of the 81st Airborne AA Battalion can be seen at the far right.

Hill 30. On the way there, it ran into retreating Fallschirmjäger, who reported that Hill 30 had been abandoned by Ost-Bataillon.439. At dusk, it joined the defensive positions of FJR.6 south of Carentan while waiting for the remainder of the regiment to arrive.

Brigadeführer Ostendorff's plan was to strike from the Meutis–Donville area between the Baupte–Carentan and Périers–Carentan roads toward Pommenauque, then attack into Carentan from the northwest corner. He presumed that the US forces on Hill 30 would withdraw once the Germans cut off the Saint-Côme-du-Mont–Carentan causeway. Ostendorff planned to conduct the initial attack without a preliminary artillery bombardment, favoring surprise. The main force, I./SS-Pz.Gren.Regt.37, was assigned to advance on the left side of the highway, and Tetzmann's 6./SS-Pz.Gren. Regt.37 on the right. Ostendorff arrogantly assumed that his untested troops would capture Carentan, and asked von der Heydte whether they should follow it up by turning east to capture Isigny or west to seize Sainte-Mère-Église.

Gen. Taylor expected that the most likely avenue of a German attack would be from the southwest due to the terrain, as was indeed the case. The area west of the Carentan–Baupte road was elevated and dry before reaching the Prairies Marécageuses de Gorges, a large marshland. The area east of the road on either side of the Canal de Vire et Taute was flooded. As a result, Taylor deployed the 506th PIR in an arc from the Carentan–Baupte road up to the flooded area where the railroad line reached Pommenauque, supported by nine M5A1 light tanks of Co. D, 70th Tank Battalion. The 501st PIR was deployed on the southern side of the road in the La Billonnerie–Hill 30 sector. The plan for June 13 was for both regiments to conduct their advance toward the southwest.

Another view of the same scene on the N171 Carentan–Périers road where three StuG IV assault guns were knocked out on the afternoon of June 13. A 6-pdr (57mm) antitank gun of the 81st Airborne AA Battalion can be seen on the right, while behind it is the second of the three knocked-out German assault guns.

Both the German and American attacks began shortly after dawn. Johnson's 501st PIR was halted immediately by heavy machine-gun fire as it quickly collided into the advancing 6./SS-Pz.Gren.Regt.37. It held its positions for the remainder of the day, fighting back repeated German attacks.

The 506th PIR also began advancing, but by 0600hrs had started to encounter the main body of the German attack, the I./SS-Pz.Gren.Regt.37, spearheaded by StuG IV assault guns advancing along the highway. Initially, the 2/506th forces consisted of Co. D on the right, Co. F on the left, and Co. E in reserve. Co. F, nearer the road, was hit hard by the main body of the Germans' combined infantry/armored vehicle attack. The fighting was extremely chaotic, as the area was broken up into small bocage-lined fields. Co. F fell back about 150 yards to the reserve line near a farm building being used as the battalion command post. This exposed the flank of Co. D and threatened to collapse the 2/506th defenses. Winter's Co. E then advanced, trying to close the gap.

The paratroopers did not have many antitank weapons, except for a small number of bazookas and antitank rifle grenades. The M5A1 light tanks from D/70th Tank Battalion only arrived around 0800hrs. The StuG IVs from SS-Panzer.Abt.17 knocked out one M5A1 light tank almost immediately. The light tanks were too few in number, and too poorly armed and armored, to deal with the StuG IV assault guns. However, they did prove useful in knocking out German machine-gun nests. In the Co. F sector, Harry "Dutch" Ostrander, a rifle grenadier, lobbed a few rifle grenades at a StuG IV, getting a lucky hit when one fell on top of the loader, who had his hatch open while firing the roof MG42 machine gun. The grenade dropped inside the vehicle, killing the crew and disabling the vehicle. In Co. E, Lt. Harry Welsh and Pvt. McGrath knocked out another one using a 2.36in bazooka.

With the 2/506th PIR in danger of being overrun, Col. Sink requested reinforcements. Gen. Taylor assigned Chapuis' 2/502nd PIR, which arrived around 1000hrs. Aerial support came in the form of a few passes by P-47 Thunderbolts, but the weather was dismal and rainy, limiting the amount of air support possible. By this time, Taylor was aware that reinforcements from the 2nd Armored Division were approaching the scene, and he informed his forward commanders to hold on until they arrived.

At 0950hrs, the I./SS-Pz.Gren.Regt.37 reported: "Attack at a standstill in front of Carentan. Enemy attacking from Carentan with tanks." By 1045hrs, the situation had deteriorated further: "Forced to withdraw under massive enemy pressure." By noon, the momentum of the German attack was spent. Von der Heydte later described the situation:

> Severe fighting raged from hedge to hedge, at close quarters and hand-to-hand. The Fallschirmjäger nevertheless succeeded in gaining several hundred meters of terrain north of the railroad embankment while the SS Panzergrenadiers were stopped cold in unfamiliar terrain where observation was obstructed. The exercise of command in such terrain is extremely difficult. During the fighting, the SS units became disorganized. The commanders, no longer masters of the situation, lost control of their units to an increasing degree. Communications were disrupted at one location or another. Gaps developed that the enemy skillfully infiltrated. At one farm, the division commander himself was engaged in close combat for several minutes with enemy troops who had broken through. In short, by 1200, it was obvious that the attack on Carentan had failed.

The farm mentioned by von der Heydte was possibly the one fought over by Lt. Ronald Speirs and the 2nd Platoon, Co. D, 506th PIR, and later recounted in postwar study at the Fort Benning Infantry School. As the German assault was gradually halted, the US forces planned a counterattack.

The Enigma leak

Allied intelligence had learned of the transfer of the 17.SS-Pz.Gren.Div. to the Carentan area on June 11 due to an Ultra decrypt of a German Enigma radio transmission. The German Heer and Waffen-SS maintained good communication security by relying on field telephones and ground lines that could not be intercepted. The weak link was the Luftwaffe. Most of the Panzer divisions had a Luftwaffe Flivo (Fliegerverbindungsoffizier: Air Liaison Officer) attached. These officers usually communicated with higher headquarters via radio, with the messages encrypted by Enigma machines. Allied counterintelligence intercepted a Flivo message on June 12 requesting air support for an attack in the Carentan area that day. Senior Allied commanders were immediately warned of this threat, though the attack did not occur on June 12. Additional messages were intercepted around midnight on June 12/13, indicating that the attack had been rescheduled for June 13. The Flivo requested aerial reconnaissance in the Carentan area as well as bomber attacks on Carentan in the predawn hours in preparation for the attack. The Ultra decrypts were passed on to only a very small group of senior commanders. Bradley's First US Army (FUSA) received the information via a Special Liaison Unit (SLU) reporting to Col. Benjamin "Monk" Dickson, the army's G-2. Dickson then briefed Bradley on the information.

At 0005hrs on June 13, shortly after receiving the Ultra decrypt, Dickson informed Bradley of the details, indicating that the 17.SS-Pz.Gren.Div. would stage an attack against Carentan that morning. At the time, the only FUSA armored reserve was Brig. Gen. Maurice Rose's Combat Command A (CCA) of 2nd Armored Division in the V Corps sector assisting the 29th Infantry Division around Isigny. Bradley contacted the V Corps commander, Maj. Gen. Gerow, and told him to mobilize a CCA task force with a battalion each of tanks and infantry to deal with the threat.

That night, Brig. Gen. Norman Cota, the assistant commander of the 29th Infantry Division, reported to V Corps that he had spotted 150 German troops entering the town of Montmartin-en-Graignes, located between Isigny and Carentan. This message was garbled and misunderstood as "150 tanks." This created confusion about the direction of the attack, since the Ultra decrypts suggested that the German attack would be directed at the western side of Carentan, not from the eastern side. As a result of these uncertainties, the CCA task force was directed to an assembly area near Le Veys, between Isigny and Carentan and immediately north of Montmartin-en-Graignes.

The 2nd Armored Division decided to organize a more robust task force than Bradley's initial instructions. Rose assigned the 1/66th and 2/66th Armored Regiment, 3/41st Armored Infantry Regiment, and 14th Armored Field Artillery Battalion to the mission. The task force was under the command of Col. John Collier, though Rose accompanied the column. The units began to move out around 0315hrs and arrived in the Le Veys assembly area by 0630hrs. Patrols were dispatched down local roads to

Col. John Collier (right) consults with Brig. Gen. Maurice Rose (left) during the advance by CCA, 2nd Armored Division, toward Carentan.

CCA, 2nd Armored Division, counterattack outside Carentan, afternoon of June 13

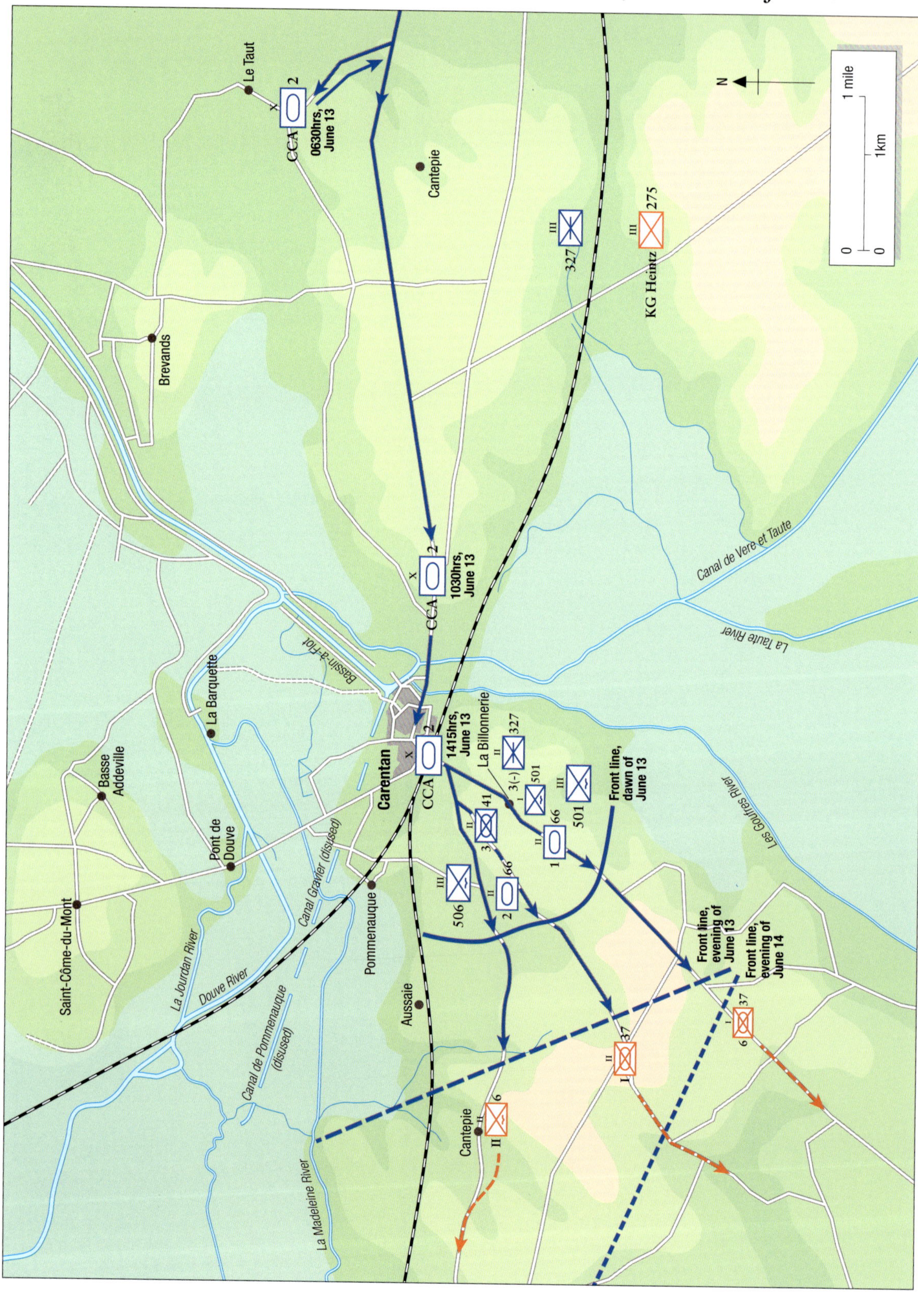

the south toward Montmartin-en-Graignes, where the German attack was anticipated.

The sector east of Carentan was held by Col. Joseph Harper's 327th GIR. Shortly after dawn, an officer from Bradley's FUSA headquarters arrived at Harper's command post, and informed Harper that there was a battalion of tanks and armored infantry at his disposal to deal with the German threat. Harper was puzzled why he would need such a force, because the situation was under control. Contacting Taylor in Carentan, it became obvious that a mistake had been made. Taylor informed the FUSA officer that the Germans were attacking on the west side of Carentan, not the east, and the reinforcements were desperately needed there.

As a result, the CCA task force was ordered to advance to Carentan by 1030hrs. Upon arriving at an apple orchard on the eastern outskirts of the town, Rose, Collier, and Taylor met to discuss the operation. The plan was to conduct a two-pronged attack by the task force from the northwest corner of Carentan.

The American riposte

The right flank of the CCA attack consisted of the 2/66th Armored and 3/41st Armored Infantry. The attack began at 1415hrs and passed through the 506th PIR, heading down the Carentan–La Campagne road used earlier by the German attack force. Paratroopers boarded some of the M4 medium tanks of the 2/66th Armored and took advantage of their turret-mounted .50 cal heavy machine guns to fire on the Germans. Lt. Donald Critchfield, a tank platoon leader in Co. I, 66th Armored, later recalled his impressions of the paratroopers: "They were an angry bunch... [They] quickly boarded our tanks and quickly exhausted our supply of .50 caliber ammo. I've never seen so many dead – before or since."

Capt. Cameron Warren, who led Co. H, 66th Armored, further described the day's fighting:

> The attack jumped off in a blinding rainstorm, supported by our airborne troops. Our paratroopers are positively magnificent fighting men – in my opinion, the best in the business. The Krauts were launching an attack of their own when we hit them. The situation was very critical. For our boys in the tanks, it was their first trip to the plate – a few saw some action in Sicily. The fight was to the death for both sides, and extremely bitter fighting. The Boche had played some underhanded tricks and nobody was in much mood to take prisoners. Very few were taken by either side. After six hours of steady but slow progress, we reached our objectives and the attack was extremely successful.

At the same time, the 1/66th Armored, with two battalions of the 502nd PIR and 1/401st GIR, advanced down the Carentan–Périers road. The after-action report of the CCA later recalled:

> The attack was made against extremely heavy resistance, hampered by rain and poor visibility, and over terrain most unfavorable to tank action. Enemy mortar concentrations, anti-tank gun, and tank gun fire were encountered. Each hedgerow presented a formidable obstacle to tanks and offered ideal cover and concealment to the fanatically aggressive enemy. Many cases were

A meeting of General der Flieger Eugen Meindl (far left), commander of II.Fallschirmjäger-Korps, von der Heydte, and Brigadeführer Werner Ostendorff (far right) in Normandy in mid-June 1944. The young officer to Ostendorff's left was Meindl's aide. At a meeting on June 14, Meindl quashed Ostendorff's attempt to court-martial von der Heydte after the failed counterattack by the 17.SS-Pz.Gren.Div.

noted where small groups of the enemy left the cover of hedgerow and charged the advancing tanks with hand-grenades and anti-tank grenade launchers [Panzerfaust]. This type of opposition rendered our supporting infantry relatively ineffective and caused the tanks to expend enormous quantities of [machine-gun] ammunition considering the relatively short distance covered by the attack... The action consisted of a series of concerted attacks by groups of infantry and tanks no larger than a platoon, with each hedgerow, each field, each sunken road, and objective to be taken, mopped up and secured before the advance could be continued.

An M4A1 named "Giant" of Co. G, 66th Armored Regiment, moving to the embarkation area in southern England for transport to France on June 8. This tank served with CCA, 2nd Armored Division, during the fighting for Carentan on June 13–14.

The American counterattack shattered the German offensive. Von der Heydte later described the scene:

> The casualties among the SS units were unusually high. The fighting spirit of the inexperienced troops was weakened and an ever-increasing number of individual SS soldiers as well as whole groups straggled to the rear. So the FJR.6 commander [von der Heydte] had to instruct his adjutant [Hauptmann Pelser] to check the fleeing SS forces and assemble them in the vicinity of the regimental command post. In some instances, the adjutant was compelled to enforce this order at the point of a gun.

In the midst of the afternoon retreat of I./SS-Pz.Gren.Regt.37, von der Heydte used his uncommitted III./FJR.6 to create a defensive line. He encountered the commander of I./SS-Pz.Gren.Regt.37, SS-Sturmbannführer Christian Reinhardt, on the road, describing him as "dazed." Under the circumstances, von der Heydte declared that the SS battalion would be placed under his command and withdrawn further southward to more defensible positions. The new line was on either side of the N171 Carentan–Périers road, extending from the edge of the Prairies Marécageuses de Gorges marshland to the village of Le Varimesnil, with the FJR.6 on the western side and the I./SS-Pz.Gren.Regt.37 on the eastern side. This line was about 4km south of the starting point of the attack earlier in the morning.

Ostendorff caught wind of this situation and sent the division's 1a (chief of operations), SS-Hauptsturmführer Conrad, to personally escort von der Heydte back to the divisional command post at Saint-Sébastien-de-Raids. Ostendorff, apparently seeking a suitable scapegoat for his division's poor performance that day, settled upon von der Heydte, who conveniently was not a member of the Waffen-SS. He accused von der Heydte of cowardice in the face of the enemy for ordering the withdrawal and placed him under

The 14th Armored Field Artillery Battalion provided the fire support for CCA, 2nd Armored Division, during the fighting against the 17.SS-Pz. Gren.Div. on June 13. Here, one of their M7105mm howitzer motor carriages passes through Carentan.

An M5A1 light tank of the Headquarters Company, CCA, 2nd Armored Division, passing through Carentan.

arrest. That night, von der Heydte was sent before an SS military judge for court martial based on his actions that day, as well as his previous withdrawal order from Carentan on June 11.

Gen. Eugen Meindl, the temporary commander of 84.AK since Marcks' death on June 12, was informed of this scandal. He was personally familiar with von der Heydte from previous combat service. Meindl visited Ostendorff's command post on the morning of June 14, and after requesting a briefing on the previous day's fighting he immediately ordered von der Heydte released and returned to his regiment. He revoked the subordination of the FJR.6 to Ostendorff's division and placed the Fallschirmjäger under corps command instead. The whole sordid affair was swept under the rug.

The 2nd Armored Division estimated German losses as 500 killed and two prisoners of war. A German report by the 17.SS-Pz.Gren.Div. put casualties through June 15 as 79 killed, 61 missing, and 316 wounded – about half the Panzergrenadiers involved. The I./SS-Pz.Gren.Regt.37 commander, Christian Reinhardt, later stated that 60 percent of his battalion was lost, with only 200 men on hand that evening. All the officers had been killed except his adjutant and two company commanders. At least six StuG IVs were lost, as well as at least one Marder tank destroyer and one R35 light tank of Pz-Ers.u.Ausb. Abt.100. By this date, FJR.6 had been reduced to only 1,200 men, about a quarter of its original strength; most of its casualties had been suffered during the fighting from June 7–11. Losses in CCA, 2nd Armored Division were eight men killed, 45 wounded, as well as three M4 medium tanks and one M5A1 light tank lost. Co. D, 70th Tank Battalion lost one M5A1 light tank. Casualties in the 101st Airborne Division that day included 24 killed, but the number of wounded was uncertain due to inconsistencies in records.

On June 14, the US forces west of Carentan continued the advance to the southwest. CCA, 2nd Armored Division advanced into the staging area of the German attack in an arc from Baupte to Méautis. These positions were taken over later in the day by elements of the 101st Airborne Division. On the right flank, the 82nd Airborne Division reached Baupte in the late afternoon, creating a solid front southwest of Carentan.

AFTERMATH

There had been sporadic contact between VII Corps on Utah Beach and V Corps at Omaha Beach since June 10. The 327th GIR continued to solidify its positions on the eastern side of Carentan as part of the effort to secure Carentan. On June 12, the 29th Infantry Division seized two bridges on the Canal de Vire et Taute near Montmartin-en-Graignes due to fear that German possession of these bridges would hamper future American efforts to solidify the link between the V Corps and VII Corps. This mission was undertaken by Cos. C and E, 175th Infantry, 29th Division, led by the assistant divisional commander, Brig. Gen. Cota. The 101st Airborne contributed to the effort by

Following the capture of Carentan, the 327th GIR was deployed to the east of the town. Pvt. Russel Rumbley is shown carrying an SCR-300 walkie-talkie radio. He is armed with an M1 carbine with the normal wooden stock, not the folding stock version used in the paratrooper regiments.

committing Co. A, 327th GIR to assist the operation from the western side of the canal.

On the German side, Kampfgruppe Heintz was deployed to the sector on June 12, the units previously in the area having been sucked into the Carentan fighting and largely destroyed. This battlegroup had been formed by the 275.Infanterie-Division, consisting of Grenadier-Regiment.984, III./Artillierie-Regiment.275, plus some reconnaissance, engineer, and supply units attached. It was subsequently subordinated to the 17.SS-Pz.Gren.Div. and was gradually reinforced as elements of SS-Panzergrenadier-Regiment.38 arrived in the area.

The linking of the two beachheads was important enough that Bradley's First US Army decided to reinforce the Carentan–Isigny area with an entire corps, the newly deployed XIX Corps, commanded by Maj. Gen. Charles H. "Cowboy Pete" Corlett. On the morning of June 15, the first elements of the newly arrived 120th Infantry, 30th Division passed through the 327th GIR, heading south to push back German encroachments in the sector. The 30th Division put a quick end to the threat that KG Heintz and SS-Pz.Gren.Regt.38 posed to the eastern side of Carentan. The Wehrmacht made no further efforts to contest the Carentan–Isigny corridor, as by mid-June there were more substantial concerns, especially VII Corps' advance on Cherbourg.

The "Four Colonels of Carentan" are decorated with the Silver Star by Gen. Maxwell Taylor at a ceremony on June 15. From left to right: Lt. Col. John Michaelis, 502nd PIR; Col. Howard Johnson, 501st PIR; Col. Robert Sink, 506th PIR; and Col. Joseph Harper, 327th GIR.

The accompanying chart shows the casualties in the 101st Airborne Division in June 1944. During the first week after D-Day, the 101st Airborne had suffered higher casualties than any other US division in Normandy due to the high numbers of missing and wounded. There were several reassessments during the course of the month that led to some noticeable data inconsistencies. This was especially the case with missing men, since about half of the missing paratroopers returned to the unit by the end of the month. The division's effective strength at the end of D+8, June 14, was 8,014 men of an authorized strength of 11,036.

101st Airborne Division casualties (cumulative)

Date*		KIA	WIA	MIA	Total
D+2	Jun 8	117	482	2,237	2,836
D+3	Jun 9	157	482	2,000	2,639
D+4	Jun 10	316	1,249	1,926	3,491
D+6	Jun 12	401	1,871	1,709	3,981
D+7	Jun 13	425	1,644	1,157	3,226
D+8	Jun 14	441	1,848	1,157	3,446
D+9	Jun 15	367	1,537	2,052	3,956
D+23	Jun 29	558	1,964	1,159	3,681

**at 2400hrs*

On June 17, the 501st PIR and 327th GIR conducted limited attacks to push forward their outpost lines. These were the last significant combat actions for the 101st Airborne Division in Normandy, and the 83rd Infantry Division arrived to take its place. By the end of June, preparations began for rotation of the 101st Airborne Division back to Britain.

Lt. Gen. Omar Bradley on the podium presenting Distinguished Service Crosses to the officers of the 101st Airborne Division in June 1944. From left to right: Maj. Gen. Maxwell Taylor (divisional commander); Lt. Col. Patrick Cassidy (1/502nd PIR); Maj. Harold H. Hannah (S-3, 506th PIR); Lt. John Maloney (Chaplain, 506th PIR); Capt. Lloyd Patch (1/506th PIR); Capt. Knut Raudstein (Co. C, 506th PIR); and Lt. Richard Winters (Co. E, 506th PIR).

THE BATTLEFIELD TODAY

Probably the best-known tourist destination in the Carentan area is the Dead Man's Corner Museum, located at the actual spot of the fighting on June 7–8. It contains a significant number of artifacts relating to the 101st Airborne Division and FJR.6. There are several other museums in the area as well. The rural countryside around Saint-Côme-du-Mont has not changed greatly since the war, however the Carentan causeway, site of the fighting on June 10–11, has changed significantly since the war. In contrast to 1944, trees line the N13 road and the neighboring farm fields usually lack the wartime flooding. This requires some imagination on the part of

The Dead Man's Corner Museum is located on the spot of von der Heydte's headquarters during the fighting for Saint-Côme-du-Mont. The M5A1 is a replica of the tank knocked out during the battle that gave the road intersection its grim nickname. (Steven McCloud)

visitors to imagine the scene in June 1944. The area near Bridge No. 4 has changed considerably, being submerged by a traffic roundabout. The Ingouf farm (Férme Pommenauque) remains, but its former rural setting has been transformed by the commercial and industrial construction that completely surrounds it. Likewise, the "Bloody Gulch" area, where Co. E, 506th PIR fought on June 13, has been partially submerged under suburban sprawl.

Interest in the battle of Carentan was substantially increased by the *Band of Brothers* TV series that includes episodes devoted to the fighting by Co. E, 506th PIR at Brécourt Manor on June 6 and Carentan on June 12–13. As a result, there are usually commemorative events in Carentan around the June 6 anniversary. There have been a growing number of commemorative plaques and monuments around the town over the past decade.

FURTHER READING

There is a wealth of published and archival material dealing with the battle of Carentan. US Army historians conducted interviews with the officers and men of the 101st Airborne Division after the Normandy fighting, and these accounts can be found in the Regimental Studies series, the Combat Interviews collection, as well as derivative accounts such as Rappaport's excellent divisional history. Coverage of the paratroop regiments is far better than the glider infantry battalions. These were further reinforced by several studies done by surviving officers at the Infantry School at Fort Benning after the war. The popular success of *Band of Brothers* led to a flood of books about Dick Winters and the men of Co. E, 506th PIR.

On the German side, Fallschirmjäger-Regiment.6 is covered by several of von der Heydte's accounts. The English version of Greisser's unit history is choppy in its treatment of Carentan. There are a few autobiographical accounts by unit members, of which Pöppel's is the best; Dahm's recent book is atmospheric but incoherent. There are few archival resources on FJR.6. The 17.SS-Panzergrenadier-Division is covered in several books, and its war diary is available in published form as well as on the Bundesarchiv digital site.

Unpublished Army Reports and Studies

Blauensteiner, Oberst Ernst, *II Fallschirmjager Corps (May–June 1944)*, US Army Foreign Military Studies B-240 (1946)

Kindig, Capt. John, *The Operations of the 101st Airborne Division East of Ste. Mere Eglise 5–6 June 1944*, Infantry School, Fort Benning (1947)

Matheson, Maj. Salve, *The Operations of the 506th PIR (101st Airborne Division) in the Normandy Invasion 5–8 June 1944*, Infantry School, Fort Benning (1950)

Raudstein, Maj. Knut, *The Operation of the 1st Battalion, 506th PIR (101st Airborne Division) in the Vicinity of Carentan 5–8 June 1944*, Infantry School, Fort Benning (1949)

Schmidt, Gen. Lt. H., *The 275th Infantry Division (Dec. 1943–Jun. 1944)*, US Army Foreign Military Studies A-975 (1946)

Speirs, Capt. Ronald, *The Operation of the 2nd Platoon, D Company, 506th PIR (101st Airborne Division) in the vicinity of Carentan 11–13 June 1944*, Infantry School, Fort Benning (1949)

Von Criegern, Oberstleutnant Friedrich, *LXXXIV Corps (Jan–17 June 1944)*, US Army Foreign Military Studies B-784 (1948)

Von der Heydte, Oberst Friedrich, *A German Parachute Regiment in Normandy*, US Army Foreign Military Studies B-839 (1948)

Von der Heydte, Oberst Friedrich, *Gefechtsbericht des Fallschirm-Jäger-Regiments 6 fur die Zeit vom 6. Bis 13.Juni 1944*, Bundesarchiv RH 19/IX

Von der Heydte, Oberst Friedrich, *Gefechtsbericht von den Kämpfen des Fallsch.Jäg.Rgts. 6 während der Invasion im Juni 1944 im Raum Carentan; unterstellt der 17. SS-Div. "G.v.B.,"* Bundesarchiv RL 33/72

Airborne Operations in World War II, European Theater, USAF Historical Studies No. 97 (1957)
Combat Interviews: 101st Airborne Division in Normandy, NARA II, Record Group 407A
COMCRUDIV 7 – Rep of Ops for the Period 6/3-17/44, Invasion of Normandy, France, US Navy (1944)
A Historical Study of World War II Airborne Operations, Weapon Systems Evaluation Group (1951)
Regimental Unit Study #1: Carentan Causeway Fight (9 June–11 June 1944), Historical Division, US Army ETO
Regimental Unit Study #2: Fight at the Lock, Historical Division, US Army ETO
Regimental Unit Study #3: 506th Parachute Infantry Regiment in Normandy Drop, Historical Division, US Army ETO
Report of Operations, 66th Armored Regiment, 13–14 June 1944 Carentan, France, US Army (1944)
War Diary, USS Quincy, *Operations off Normandy Coast, June 1944*

Books and Articles

Afiero, Massimiliano, *The 17th Waffen-SS Panzergrenadier Division*, Schiffer: Atglen (2018)
Ambrose, Stephen, *Band of Brothers*, Simon & Schuster: New York (1992)
Anonymous, *Utah Beach to Cherbourg 6 June–27 June 1944*, US Army Historical Division (1947)
Bando, Mark, *101st Airborne: The Screaming Eagles at Normandy*, MBI: Osceola (1994)
Bando, Mark, *Vanguard of the Crusade: The 101st Airborne Division in World War II*, Hemdal: Bayeux (2012)
Bernage, Georges, *Objectif Carentan 6-15 juin 1944*, Heimdal: Bayeux (2010)
Bernage, Georges, *Utah Beach*, Heimdal: Bayeux (2014)
Bernage, Georges, "Von der Heydte et l'élite de ses officiers de Fallschirmajger-Regiment.6," *Normandie 1944*, No 32 (August 2019), pp.26–43
Blaker, Gordon, *Iron Knights: The US 66th Armored Regiment*, Burd Street: Shippensburg (1999)
Cazenave, Stephan and Stéphane Neuhaus, *SS-Panzer-Abteilung.17: Carentan-Periers-Poche de Roncey*, Maranes: Bayeux (2024)
Chazette, Alain, *Fallschirmjäger: Les parachutistes allemands en France 1943–1944*, Histoire & Collections: Paris (2001)
Dahms, Jo, *Du oder Ich*, BoD (2014)
De Trez, Michael, *At the Point of No Return: Pictorial History of the American Paratroopers in the Invasion of Normandy*, D-Day Publishing: Wezembeek-Oppem (1994)
Frappé, Jean-Bernard, *La Luftwaffe Face au Débarquement: Normandie 6 Juin-31 août 1944*, Heimdal: Bayeux (2018)
Gardner, Ian, *Airborne: The Combat Story of Ed Shames of Easy Company*, Osprey: Oxford (2015)
Gardner, Ian and Roger Day, *Tonight We Die as Men: The Untold Story of the 3/506th PIR*, Osprey: Oxford (2009)
Griesser, Volker, *The Lions of Carentan: Fallschirmjager Regiment 6: 1943–1945*, Casemate: Havertown (2011)
Henkemans, Niels, *Defending Normandy*, Panzerwrecks, Old Heathfield, Vol. 1A (2024); Vol 1B (2025)
Henkemans, Niels, *et al.*, "Who was the Dead Man at Dead Man's Corner?" *WWII Quarterly* (Spring 2020), pp.14–21
Hinsley, F. H., *et al.*, *British Intelligence in the Second World War, Vol. 3, Part 2*, HMSO: London (1988)
Koskimaki, George, *D-Day with the Screaming Eagles*, Casemate: Havertown (1970)
Lahey, R. J., "Hitler's Intuition, Luftwaffe Photoreconnaissance, and the Reinforcement of Normandy," *Journal of Military History* No. 86 (January 2022), pp.77–109
Longue, Matthieu, "Easy Company,2/506th PIR dans la Bataille de Carentan," *Magazine 39-45*, No. 323 (June 2014), pp.38–67
Marshall, S. L. A., *Night Drop: The American Airborne Invasion of Normandy*, Little, Brown: New York (1962)
McDonough, James and Richard S. Gardner, *Skyriders: History of the 327/401 Glider Infantry*, Battery Press: Nashville (1980)
Nauroth, H. S. and B. Steinberg, *Die Geschichte der 91.Luftlande-Division*, Tredition: Hamburg (2017)

Paich, Bernad, "Quand les Allemands inondaient le Contentin Baupte, fevrier 1944," *Magazine 39-45*, No. 264 (February 2009), pp.13–15

Perrigault, Jean-Claude and R. Meister, *Gotz von Berlichingen: Normandie*, Heimdal: Bayeux (2004)

Pöppel, Martin, *Heaven & Hell: The War Diary of a German Paratrooper*, Spellmount: Staplehurst (1988)

Poyser, Tony and Bill Brown, *Fighting Fox Company*, Casemate: Havertown (2013)

Rappaport, Leonard and A. Northwood, *Rendezvous with Destiny: A History of the 101st Airborne Division*, Battery Press: Nashville (1948)

Reardon, Mark, *Defending Fortress Europe: The War Diary of the German 7th Army in Normandy*, Aberjona: Bedford (2009)

Ruge, Friedrich, *Rommel in Normandy*, Macdonald's and Jane's: London (1979)

Stober, Hans, *Combat History of the 17. SS-Panzer-Grenadier-Division Gotz Von Berlichingen, Vol.1*, Federowicz: Winnipeg (2017)

Van der Brink, Denic, *Heroes of Carentan*, Heimdal: Bayeux (2019)

Villahermosa, Gilberto, *Hitler's Paratroopers in Normandy*, Pen & Sword: Barnsley (2019)

Wind, M. and H. Günther, *Kriegstagebuch 11.SS-Panzergrenadier-Division vom 30.Oktober 1943 bis 6.Mai 1945*, Schild: Munich (1993)

INDEX

Figures in **bold** refer to illustrations.